THE LAST DISCIPLE

My Memoirs with Bruce Lee

Peter Chin

Copyright © 2024, Peter Chin

This book is an independent compilation and is not associated with or authorized, licensed, sponsored or endorsed by any person or entity affiliated with the well-known artists, performers, labels or companies referenced in this book. All trademarks are the property of their respective owners. Such trademarks are used for editorial purposes only, and the publisher makes no claim of ownership and shall acquire no right, title, or interest in such trademarks by virtue of this publication.

With the exception of outstanding and prevailing copyrights held on the original source material, the copyright on the selection, composition, restoration, translations, remastering and authorship of this publication belong to Peter Chin © 2023 All rights reserved.

No parts of this publication may be reproduced or transmitted in any form or by any means, graphic, electronic or mechanical, including photocopying, recording, or by any information storage and retrieval system, without prior premission.

Publishing support provided by
Ignite Press
55 Shaw Ave. #204
Clovis, CA 93612
www.IgnitePress.us

ISBN: 979-8-9896588-0-0
ISBN: 979-8-9896588-1-7 (Hardcover)
ISBN: 979-8-9896588-2-4 (E-book)

For bulk purchases and for booking, contact:

Peter Chin
thelastdisciplebook@gmail.com
www.peterchin.com

Because of the dynamic nature of the Internet, web addresses or links contained in this book may have been changed since publication and may no longer be valid. The content of this book and all expressed opinions are those of the author and do not reflect the publisher or the publishing team. The author is solely responsible for all content included herein.

Library of Congress Control Number: 2023923704

FIRST EDITION

For Bruce.

For my wife Sandy, my two daughters Jade and Crystal, and my grandchildren Amelia and Jaden.

— *Peter Chin*

For Bruce and my late sifu Ted Wong.

For my wife Sherry and my two sons, Derek and Darin.

— *Tommy Gong*

TABLE OF CONTENTS

Foreword by Linda Lee Cadwell..........................vii
Foreword by Ang Lee....................................ix
Foreword by Javier Mendez..............................xi
About the Author/About the Collaborator...............xiii
Introduction...xv

Chapter 1   Growing Up in Hong Kong, Arriving in America...1
Chapter 2   Bruce Is the One!...........................9
Chapter 3   Meeting at 20th Century Fox................13
Chapter 4   The First Lesson...........................17
Chapter 5   Bruce's Devastating Kicks..................21
Chapter 6   Bruce's Blinding Speed and Cat-Like Reflexes...29
Chapter 7   After Training — a Close, Personal Bond Forms...35
Chapter 8   From Light as a Swallow to Honest Expression...39
Chapter 9   The Perfect Move: Intercepting.............43
Chapter 10 The Unity of Mind and Body.................45
Chapter 11 Bruce Lee: Reel or Real Fighter............47
Chapter 12 Physical Conditioning and Jogging..........51
Chapter 13 Bruce's Back Injury........................61
Chapter 14 Bruce as a Teacher.........................63
Chapter 15 Bruce's Intelligence and Photographic Memory...67
Chapter 16 Jeet Kune Do — the Enigma..................69
Chapter 17 Martial Arts Philosophy for Life...........75

Chapter 18   Hanging Around with Bruce in Hollywood......81
Chapter 19   Bruce's Charisma, Magnetism and Humor......89
Chapter 20   Struggling in Hollywood....................93
Chapter 21   Success and Loneliness in Hong Kong.........97
Chapter 22   The Aftermath............................105
Chapter 23   Fifty Years Later.........................109
Chapter 24   Why Did Bruce Give Me a JKD Certificate?.....115

Conclusion: Bruce's True Secret....................119
Acknowledgments..................................123

FOREWORD BY LINDA LEE CADWELL

Are you curious about Bruce Lee as a man and a friend apart from his film and martial arts fame? In this book by Peter Chin and Tommy Gong, you will experience a perspective that is unique and personal. Peter relates little-known stories about Bruce, his martial arts study and his film career. But what sets this book apart is the very special relationship between two friends — Bruce and Peter.

I have known Peter since he first met Bruce in 1967. That means that Peter and I have been friends for nearly 60 years, and it goes without saying that I know Peter's heart when it comes to his friendship with Bruce. Peter was a fixture in our house on many occasions and at all hours of the day. While Bruce taught many students and formed friendships with them, Peter was in a special category. Bruce considered Peter to be more of a friend than a martial arts student, even though Peter did study the art. They were able to converse in Cantonese, and so many of their conversations were about personal things, such as their childhood in Hong Kong, growing up under the rule of foreign powers, being inspired by the same books, and certain philosophical thoughts better expressed in Chinese than English. You will experience intimate details about the mind and heart of Bruce Lee not recorded elsewhere.

Peter would be the first to admit that since he moved around a lot in his formative years, his English is not perfect. With the help of Tommy Gong, Peter has found a way to tell the world about a man he held in high esteem. Peter and Tommy have shared a friendship based on their respect for Bruce and his art of *jeet kune do*. It adds depth to the story that they are both Chinese and can translate and interpret certain concepts that may be abstract to those of us who are not Chinese. Tommy is proficient in jeet kune do and has written extensively on the art. (See *Bruce Lee: The Evolution of a Martial Artist* by Tommy Gong.) Because of his exposure to the art and his rapport with Peter, Tommy was able to put Peter's words and memories into a fascinating story.

One of the first things people think of when they hear the name Bruce Lee is his magnetic charisma and fierce fighting style that emanates from the screen. Others may know him as a philosopher whose teachings have inspired people to better their lives. Where did his magic and wisdom come from? In this book, Peter and Tommy give us more clues to Bruce Lee, a man who said, "You know what I think of myself? As a human being."

— Linda Lee Cadwell,
Bruce Lee's wife

FOREWORD BY ANG LEE

There have been many books written about Bruce Lee and *jeet kune do* over the years, but rarely do they have the same kind of affectionate simplicity as this one. Reading it feels less like a book and more like a conversation with a friend. There is a certain innocence and love to Peter's words that gives the impression that Bruce is right there in the room with you. Such a sense of intimacy could only come from a real and personal bond of friendship, and it offers a precious insight into the living presence of Bruce Lee and his art.

What I found most interesting were the chapters on jeet kune do and Bruce's teaching method. Since Bruce's untimely passing, many people have become fixated on the idea of an "original jeet kune do," but Peter's perspective illuminates the simple fact that the art of jeet kune do is always evolving, ever expressing the individual martial artist, and the only "original" is Bruce himself. However, Bruce did not want to be imitated; he wanted his students to become authentic themselves.

His strategy of teaching sought to help each student break down their own unique walls and barriers to genuine self-expression and to continue to evolve and grow along their own paths. Bruce was a master at figuring out each of his students and guiding them in the way that was best suited to their individual needs. This personal and attentive care is what inspired such love and dedication from his students and friends, as you can see in the pages of this book.

Jeet kune do is not just about learning how to fight but also how to live. Bruce sought to develop his students not just into formidable martial artists but also, and perhaps more importantly, into artists of life.

Ang Lee,
Academy Award-winning director

FOREWORD BY JAVIER MENDEZ

This book provides amazing insights into the legend Bruce Lee's life from his pupil and friend.

— Javier Mendez,
Legendary MMA trainer

INTRODUCTION

By Peter Chin

I first heard Bruce Lee's name in 1961 and met him briefly in 1963, I really got to know Bruce for the six years between 1967 and 1973. I became his student in late 1967, and he has been the biggest influence on my life. Not one day passes by that I don't think about Bruce. Somehow his teachings keep coming up to influence me. He is always in my mind and heart.

My writings and thoughts only apply to my own experience with Bruce — what he said and taught me. And my opinions are strictly my own.

Bruce once told me: In your lifetime if you can raise your hand and say I have this many friends (five), you are an extremely lucky person.

I am also extremely blessed to have another friend besides Bruce whom I met after Bruce passed away, my current friend and spouse Sandy. As of this writing, we have been married for 43 years. Together, we have two daughters, one granddaughter and one grandson. We have lived an extremely interesting life and experienced things that others may find hard to understand.

It has been 50 years since Bruce passed, but it seems like just yesterday. Bruce's teachings continue to inspire me today. Please indulge me as I reflect on my memories with Bruce Lee.

By Tommy Gong

Bruce Lee has been a huge influence in my life. Growing up in California's Central Valley, my family was the only Chinese in our town. Bruce Lee, the only prominent Asian actor in the movies, was a childhood hero to me. I became a student of *jeet kune do* while attending college, then a board member of the Jun Fan Jeet Kune Do Nucleus/Bruce Lee Foundation contributing to his legacy for future generations. I have learned so much from him and continue to do so. At first, it was from his physical prowess, good looks, and style, but as I studied his life and writings, he has been an inspiration to me throughout my life as a child, teenager, adult, and parent.

It was in 2010 when I connected with Peter Chin in San Francisco at the 70th anniversary of Bruce Lee's life. Just after that meeting, I received the news that my *sifu* Ted Wong had passed away. It so happened that Peter was part of the same group as my late sifu's who privately trained with Bruce during the later developments of jeet kune do. In many ways, Peter helped me recover from the grief of losing my sifu and provided me with valuable information for my book *Bruce Lee: The Evolution of a Martial Artist*. Over the years, we have become close friends.

During our discussions, Peter mentioned how Bruce gave him "a diploma" for training with him on his birthday. He treasured it since it stated that he "had been personally taught by Bruce Lee." I asked, "Wait a minute, what exactly does it say at the top?" Jeet kune do was at the top of the certificate. In my research on the history of Bruce Lee and jeet june do, there were very few people who received a JKD certificate from Bruce Lee. Its recipients not only trained privately with Bruce during his later years but also cultivated close friendships with him.

Although Peter trained with Bruce Lee at the same time as Ted Wong and Herb Jackson, he had a different relationship with Bruce. Sifu Ted was the consummate student of the art; Peter had a different bond with Bruce — coming from Hong Kong, Peter attended the same school Bruce attended as well as studied *wing chun gung fu* before leaving Hong Kong. Last, Bruce and Peter would regularly communicate in Cantonese, their native tongue. As a result, Peter hung out with Bruce "shooting the bull" and shopping on Melrose Avenue, even purchasing a kaftan at the same time Bruce did.

I have found that Peter has a very deep love for Bruce, a brotherly bond that began in late 1967 when they met again on the 20th Century Fox studio lot. He was devastated when Bruce passed away, so much so that Peter attended both of Bruce's funerals — Hong Kong and Seattle. Peter was one of the six pallbearers at the Seattle funeral.

In this book, you will discover a side of Bruce Lee that very few people experienced. Enjoy!

1

GROWING UP IN HONG KONG, ARRIVING IN AMERICA

I was born in Shanghai in 1947, but my family moved to Hong Kong when I was 2 years old. My father worked for Pan American Airlines and was stationed in Japan; he would usually come back to Hong Kong for the weekend. I remember he would bring Kobe steak back to Hong Kong on occasion. My mother was a homemaker, taking care of my older brother, my three sisters, and me. We lived in Tsim Sha Tsui on the Kowloon side.

I went to Kowloon Tong Elementary School, which was located on the same street as Bruce Lee's house in the '70s. During those years, I was very active in track after school. I recall we always completed 30 minutes of exercise before entering the classroom. I will never forget the first lesson in school. The teacher wrote on the board that we must show respect to our great-grandparents, our grandparents, our parents, and our siblings, anyone who's older than us — our elders. Never talk back to your elders; even today, I have continued to follow that teaching. In 1961, I enrolled in St. Francis Xavier College, the same school Bruce attended before leaving for America.

In the early '60s in Hong Kong, families went to nightclubs for dinner and dancing. Since there was no age limit to attend nightclubs, it was a very fun time for families. Live bands performed Latin music, which was popular at the time. My fondness for dance started here, and I learned cha-cha, bossa nova, and pachanga from a Philippine Latin dancing teacher in Hong Kong.

In those days, my favorite pastime was reading Chinese martial arts storybooks, especially those by Jin Yong (**金庸**, Gum Yoong in Cantonese), a famous Chinese martial arts novelist who co-founded Ming Pao, a Hong Kong daily newspaper in 1959. I was a fan of Jin's popular *Legend of the Condor Heroes* series, a *wuxia* novel — a genre of Chinese fiction that is centered around martial arts, chivalry, and heroism. Many of his works have been adapted into films and TV shows in Hong Kong. I would later find out that Bruce was also a fan of these novels.

Although Bruce had already left for America, his reputation remained as a premier fighter in Hong Kong. His defeat of a British boxer and his wing chun skills were legendary among the young, impressionable students at St. Francis Xavier College. Stories of the rooftop fights between the wing chun and *choy li fut* schools remained fresh, and I heard from other schoolmates that with only three months of wing chun training, Bruce Lee was unbeatable alongside his wing chun senior Wong Shun Leung during street fights in Kowloon City (**九龍城**) and on the rooftops. These stories convinced me to study wing chun gung fu.

Wing chun gung fu was known to be a simplified system that a person could learn in a short time. The style has only three forms *(siu nim tau, chum kiu* and *biu ji)*, two weapons *(baat jaam dou,* or parallel-shaped double knives, and *luk dim boon gwan,* or 6½ long pole) and the famous *muk yan jong* (wooden dummy). I found it very easy to pick up and fun to practice chi sao (sticking hands), which is, in my opinion, the most important part of wing chun. It is the connection and interaction between teacher and student. It is estimated that a person can learn the whole system in two years. However, to be good at it is a completely different story. It all depends on each individual and how much time he or she spends practicing and training. As the saying goes, "What you put in is what you are going to get out."

My brother and I were very fortunate to begin learning wing chun under Chu Shong Tin, among the most respected senior students of Yip Man in Hong Kong. The class was taught on the rooftop where Chu was living in Mongkok on the Kowloon side of Hong Kong. Besides teaching wing chun, Chu also worked as secretary of the Hong Kong and Kowloon Restaurant Workers Union, which is how he met Yip Man in 1949.

Chu Shong Tin was a very soft-spoken and gentle person. During my six months of training from late 1961 to early 1962, I learned siu nim tau and chum kiu and did a lot of chi sao practice with Chu. During those days, I attended class three nights a week, each class lasting about an hour. Chu would always cover each move of the form in detail, including its intended purpose. During the following months, we completed the siu nim tau form and started to practice chi sao with Chu.

There were only five or six students during the class, so everyone received a lot of personal attention from Chu. By month four, we finished the chum kiu form and continued to practice a lot of chi sao with Chu. I noticed that he never attacked; he was always on defense. I truly believe that was his personality or his philosophy, reflecting the old maxim, "Gung fu is for self-defense."

When it comes to learning wing chun or any martial art style, it is crucial to select a teacher who dedicates ample time to working with you. For instance, in the case of wing chun, does the teacher engage in chi sao practice with you in every class? If not, how much can you realistically learn? Similarly, when attending seminars, it is essential to ensure you will have the opportunity to practice with the seminar's instructor. I will also stay away from any teacher who claims they are the original because they are still in the box.

A case in point is Chu Shong Tin, whose school experienced a decline in students because he stopped personally engaging in chi sao with his students for a period. However, after resuming chi sao practice with his students after a year, word spread, and his school became bustling once again."

Consider this significant topic: when the teacher engages in brief 5 to 10 minute workout sessions with each student, the student not only learns and improves their understanding but also gains a stronger sense of accomplishment. Simultaneously, the teacher also enjoys physical benefits from these interactions.

This subject holds considerable significance, and it played a role in Bruce's decision to close his Los Angeles school. To illustrate the point, just imagine the contrast between practicing Chi Sao with Bruce compared to practicing it with Ted or Herb.

Back in the day, it was highly desirable for parents in Hong Kong to send their children out of the country for education because there was not much work available for young people to start their careers and make a living in Hong Kong. Studying abroad allowed them to establish themselves in new worlds and become gainfully employed. In early 1963, I moved to Sydney for schooling, then landed in San Francisco in September with $200 in my pocket, just like Bruce did when he first arrived in America (he started with only $100).

My older brother was already in the U.S., so we lived together. I was on a student visa and had to work to support myself. One of my brother's Hong Kong schoolmates was Howard Tso, and along with his sister Pearl, they were both close friends of Bruce. Their father, Tso Tat Wah, was in show business along with Bruce's father, Lee Hoi-Chuen. Bruce, Howard, Pearl, and my brother used to socialize together back in those days in Hong Kong. Howard moved to London, but they kept in touch occasionally.

A few months later, my brother received a call from Howard who told him that Bruce was teaching gung fu in Oakland. Bruce was staying at James Lee's home. He suggested paying Bruce a visit to say hello. My brother asked if I wanted to tag along and meet Bruce Lee. Since I heard so much about Bruce in Hong Kong, I said, "Of course!"

We arrived at James' house in Oakland. James was a traditional gung fu practitioner who gave up the "classical mess" to become Bruce's second instructor at his Jun Fan Gung Fu Institute. When we walked in, approximately 10 students were lined up side by side about a few feet apart, all facing Bruce, who was showing them some punches. Bruce stopped and waved to James to continue teaching as he greeted us. We conversed in Cantonese about what we were doing in America. I mentioned to Bruce my intention to move to Los Angeles next year, to which he mentioned that Ed Parker is hosting the first International Karate Championships and that he was invited to perform a demonstration. He suggested that if I have the chance, I should go and watch his demonstration, and I responded, "I sure will be there". During that meeting, my first impression of Bruce was that he was kind of cocky or arrogant but that he knew what he was talking about and could back up what he said. This was December 1963; it would be another nine months before I saw Bruce in Long Beach.

Peter dancing

Bruce Lee dancing   Peter's parents 1963

James wrote in Chinese "Lee 8 Legs" "Practice kung fu hard" "James"

Bruce Lee with Tso Tat Wah, father of Howard and Pearl

2

BRUCE IS THE ONE!

I attended the event in August 1964 for one reason and one reason only. The fact that Ed Parker put on the first major martial arts tournament in the United States mattered very little to me. There were many leading martial artists present, but there was only one person I wanted to see: Bruce Lee.

When I first landed in America, I had already met Bruce in Oakland, California, at James Lee's home. James Yimm Lee was a prominent martial artist in the San Francisco Bay Area. When I told Bruce that I was moving to Los Angeles, he mentioned that he was invited to put on a demonstration at Ed Parker's first International Karate Championships in Long Beach, California, and if I had the time, I should go and watch him.

It was a warm day in Long Beach, or at least in the convention center since there were many people in attendance combined with the physical activity taking place. Many karate practitioners wore their *gi* or uniform. Bruce wore a black traditional *gung fu* uniform. Toward the end of the day, one by one, the martial arts masters began to demonstrate their respective styles and techniques. Bruce was the last to perform.

Bruce was in a class of his own — multiple levels above the previous martial artists. His movements were much more dynamic and faster than any previous practitioner. Everything Bruce did was impeccable, and he was supremely confident. His charisma was like a magnet. He demonstrated two-finger push-ups, the efficiency of his technique and *chi sao,* which I was familiar with because of my previous *wing chun gung fu* training, but when Bruce did the one-inch punch, I was shocked and impressed. BRUCE IS THE ONE!

It looked so simple and minute, almost imperceptible yet destructive! Bruce placed his fist on the chest of his volunteer, and in an instant, the volunteer's chest violently compressed backward, his feet lifted off the floor and he flew backward into the chair conveniently placed behind. A close-range technique, it was completely different from the way Hollywood portrayed a powerful punch, typically starting out in left field (as the saying goes). Bruce was able to concentrate all his speed and power through just one single move from the bottom of his feet, through his body, and into his fist at the precise moment of impact — a demonstration of body mechanics, timing, and precision. I will never forget it; it is burned into my memory.

I made it my mission to train and learn from him. Little did I know that I would become Bruce's last disciple.

Bruce's one-inch punch — I will never forget it.

3

MEETING AT 20ᵀᴴ CENTURY FOX

In 1964, I moved to Los Angeles to attend school and worked as a busser to support myself. In those days, the only jobs available for Chinese were either working in a restaurant or doing laundry work. The restaurant I worked at was called Madame Wu's Garden, considered a celebrity restaurant in Santa Monica, California. I had the chance to serve celebrities like Doris Day, Cary Grant, Frank Sinatra, Mia Farrow, Elizabeth Taylor, Robert Redford, and many others. In 1966, I was working as a bellhop at the Century Plaza Hotel in Century City. I always had two jobs because I worked as a screen extra occasionally.

Since I liked dancing, I took about six months of modern jazz dance and a few months of ballet in Los Angeles during this time. I was interested in show business, so I joined the Screen Extras Guild and started to get some work on TV shows and movies. For instance, I was an extra in Alfred Hitchcock's *Torn Curtain* with Paul Newman and Julie Andrews and *The Green Berets* with John Wayne as a Vietnamese soldier. I recall John Wayne arriving on the set by helicopter each morning. I soon got a Screen Actors Guild card with the help of famed director Robert Wise because he selected me for a small speaking part (with Cantonese lines) at the end of the movie *The Sand Pebbles*. I was the young man who ran to the temple at the end of the movie informing the cast that the Chinese soldiers were on their way. Of course, my character dies right after it is interesting that I would meet Steve McQueen, the star of the movie, by way of Bruce later on.

Around this same time, there was news that Bruce would be in *The Green Hornet* TV series, but I did not contact him because I felt like we were on different levels — he was a co-star, and I was just an extra on the set. I also heard Bruce was teaching celebrities, charging $100 an hour. As a bellhop, there was no way I could afford the lessons.

In late 1967, I was an extra on the original Star Trek TV series. During a break, I walked out of the studio set and I saw Bruce was outside the studio. I quickly walked over to say hello in Cantonese, and I was glad to see him. I told Bruce that I saw his demonstration in Long Beach and that I would really like to learn gung fu from him. Knowing that Bruce charged quite a bit for private lessons, I told him that I could not afford the $100 an hour per lesson. To my surprise, he said to me: "Peter, this is my last week of promotions for The Green Hornet. I am starting a private class at my house next Wednesday. Come to my house and I will teach you as a friend." He gave me his phone number to call him so he could give me the address. I was shocked and excited: Wow! Was I dreaming? This is how my relationship with Bruce Lee started. I felt blessed. Despite being on different levels, Bruce accepted me as a FRIEND.

Star Trek: Peter to the right of Spock

Peter and Chuck Norris in "The Wrecking Crew"

Bruce Lee-Kato

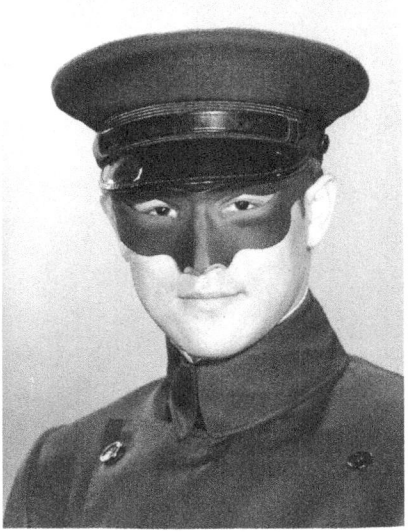

Peter, this is my last week of promotions for The *Green Hornet*. I am starting a private class at my house next Wednesday. Come to my house and I will teach you as a friend.

4

THE FIRST LESSON

I arrived at Bruce's home in Culver City, California, for my first lesson with two other students: Ted Wong and Herb Jackson. At that time Bruce would not accept any students unless they had already learned some martial arts. He did not have much patience to teach someone without some prior martial arts training. Ted and Herb started their training at the Los Angeles Chinatown school. Ted had little to no previous training but was a dedicated student who had a passion for Western boxing, which I believe Bruce found appealing. Bruce knew I studied wing chun with Chu Shong Tin because I mentioned it during our first meeting in Oakland.

When the class started, we first did some warm-up exercises. He then told Ted and Herb to put on the gear to practice sparring out on the patio. In the meantime, Bruce and I did a little chi sao; I assume he was trying to feel me out. I noticed that Bruce had the same forward energy from his arms that Chu Shong Tin emphasized to me. At the same time, Bruce's chi sao was different from Chu's since Chu seldom attacked — most of the time he was defensive. Bruce's chi sao was more offensive. After a few minutes, we stopped and headed over to where Ted and Herb were sparring.

What Is Jeet Kune Do?

I asked Bruce, "Can you explain to me why you call your gung fu *'jeet kune do'*?" We were speaking in Cantonese, standing in front of each other. He said, "OK, I am going to throw a punch at you, and you just react naturally any way you feel like it." When he punched with his left hand, I automatically raised my right hand and blocked it.

"OK, now you throw me a punch," he said. So, I threw Bruce a punch with my right hand, then I realized his left hand was in front of my face. "Now do you understand". My arm blocks your punch except I hit you at the same time. My defense is offense. Jeet kune do basically has no defense. The offense is the defense, or simply put, it is only one move; simplicity, one move only whenever you can. That is why I call it the intercepting fist in Cantonese. No defense, only offense. One move instead of two." Even today, most martial arts still have two moves instead of one. Bruce asked, "Do you understand what jeet kune do means now?" I replied, "I got it." I could easily pick up what Bruce was saying because we spoke the same language.

"Now your two hands and your two legs are your tools. You must sharpen your tools. Your body is your temple. You must learn to take care of your temple," Bruce continued. "One important thing you must remember, I can only show you the way." He placed his finger on my forehead, motioning a small cut. "What comes out from that cut will totally depend on you. In other words, I can only show you the way. The rest is up to you."

Kicking

A few minutes later, we stopped, and he asked if I practiced any kicks. I had not. Bruce proceeded to the heavy bag hanging in the room. He did a side kick to the bag, which swung really hard. Bruce then asked me to stand behind the bag and told me to brace myself. The next thing I knew, I almost hit the wall. That was the first time I felt Bruce's side kick power. I was shocked. It was much more powerful than the one-inch punch I saw in Long Beach.

Then Bruce instructed me to try kicking the bag. I kicked the bag, but it only swung a little. Bruce exclaimed that when you kick, you must get your hip into it. The power comes from your core. While he was talking, he showed me the motion of the left foot sliding toward the right foot and at the same time twisting the hip into the kick, together in one motion.

Bruce told me to kick the bag again. I kicked it as he showed me, and this time, I could really feel the difference in the power of the kick. Bruce said, "OK, you keep practicing the kick."

He went outside to do some sparring with Ted and Herb. I observed that when they sparred, their hand movements were mostly like boxing and with some kicks. Later, we all went inside, and Bruce said that is all for tonight. Ted, Herb, and I then faced Bruce while performing the salutation and the class ended.

I do not recall any of us (Ted, Herb, or I) ever missing a class. I went to school in the morning and then went to work after school. Ted and Herb probably spent more time with Bruce during the day before the regular Wednesday night class, and I probably spent more time with Bruce after the night class. We always had a great time together during these classes. There were always serious moments, and there were also fun, happy, and laughing moments, which I still cherish today. Ted and Herb were great people to have as your *si hing, or older brothers* (師兄) We really developed a brotherhood in those years.

I realized why Bruce's private class session with celebrities was worth $100 an hour. During that one hour, I learned so much from Bruce. If it were with other martial arts instructors, it might have taken many years and I would still be in the dark.

Ted Wong's Wedding: Peter, Herb, Krina, Ted, Bruce, and Linda.
"Wednesday Classmates"

My head snapped back with my feet coming off the ground
and I slammed against the wall.

5

BRUCE'S DEVASTATING KICKS

I trained with Bruce over a 30-month period beginning in late 1967. Typically, we started with some basic warm-ups, rotating our knees, squatting, circling our shoulders, stretching (Bruce always mentioned the importance of **flexibility**), and performing some sit-ups, push-ups, and other calisthenics before proceeding to basic techniques, which consisted mainly of footwork and kicking drills.

My training with Bruce did not involve trapping and what he taught in his schools back in Seattle and Oakland. Aside from practicing chi sao, basically just to warm up, there was very little emphasis on wing chun or trapping. Bruce had already evolved from it, so there was much more concentration on punching and kicking, especially sparring and conditioning.

Bruce always emphasized footwork, not only for mobility, agility, controlling distance or positioning but also to use it to generate power into one's punches and kicks. Shifting your feet and legs along with getting your hips into the movement was vital. Bruce always reminded me that power comes from your core, the abdominal group of muscles. You must get your whole body into it, starting from your feet, hips, and hands, and you only release the hit until the last second of impact in one motion to achieve real power.

Bruce would illustrate this with Newton's cradle (aka Newton's pendulum). Illustrating the conservation of momentum and energy, when a swinging sphere hits the row of spheres, the force is transferred through all of them, with only the last sphere moving and swinging up. ** (Wikipedia) This was Bruce's way of showing how the power of the kick begins with footwork, generating momentum, and the heel penetrating into the center of the target.

Why So Much Kicking?

When I was training with Bruce in Los Angeles. During his time in Los Angeles, Bruce trained his legs almost as diligently as he did his hands. In the four and a half movies he made, approximately 70% of the fight scenes focused on kicks, while the remaining 30% emphasized hand techniques and he focused on kicking in all his private teaching. Often, Bruce would tell me to practice kicking the heavy bag, including the roundhouse, spin, and high kicks but mainly the side kick.

One day, Bruce was sparring with Ted Wong and Herb Jackson out on the patio, but he told me to "just go and practice your kicks." I was a bit frustrated, and after a while, I finally asked him why he made me train so much on my kicks. He did not say a word. He walked over to the living room, sat on a chair, and stretched out his leg. He placed his arm next to his leg and said, "Do you understand now?" I instantly realized that the leg is longer and bigger than the arm, and therefore more damaging. By adding kicks, Bruce was able to increase his offensive capabilities. The damage inflicted by a kick is much more devastating than a punch.

> *"I fear not the man who has practiced **10,000 kicks** once,*
> *but I fear the man who has practiced one kick **10,000 times**."*
> —*Bruce Lee*

I was not aware of Bruce's quote back then, but it perfectly described his philosophy in martial arts. A singular focus on perfecting one technique was in his nature. Bruce did everything he could to make the side kick his most powerful weapon through constant repetition, breaking down every component, enhancing it with supplementary training, and fine-tuning its timing.

Bruce told me a fabled story, in which the young student is instructed to carry a basket of rolled paper up the hill to the monastery, and then flatten them out daily for a year. The next year, the student is instructed to flatten the paper in another way to train and condition his arms and the specific movement. In year three, another flattening method is assigned. One day, when the young student was in the village, there was something amiss and the people crowded the streets to see what was going on. The young student was also excited to see what was happening, so he put his arms in between the crowd and spread his arms open. All the people dropped like flies. I fear the man who practiced one kick 10,000 times. It is the same principle.

Kicking the Shield

Bruce's demonstrations of kicking someone holding a kicking shield are legendary. He had two shields for kicking. Herb Jackson made a larger one made of wood and foam inside. It was heavy and was fashioned with seat belts to be suspended from the shoulders. This shield was designed to absorb the kick's power so the holder would feel more of a thud when Bruce kicked it. The other was an air shield used for tackling football training. It was lightweight and portable, so Bruce liked to take it with him when traveling for private lessons.

When holding the air shield, you could really feel Bruce's power. When he was about to kick it, Bruce shuffled his feet aggressively to get his body in motion, and the generated momentum transferred into the air shield when Bruce kicked. Combined with perfect timing and body alignment, it was immensely powerful. When Bruce's kick made impact, the air in the shield violently compressed inward, so the air had to go somewhere. That would be the person on the other side holding the shield, lifting the person off his feet, and propelling him backward into the air.

In early 1968, I was having dinner with a few friends who complained about me always talking about Bruce Lee. They asked, "Is he really that good?" One friend in particular, Victor Lam, knew people in Hong Kong's show business. I answered, "Well, it's hard for me to explain how powerful his kicks are, but would you like to try feeling them?" Victor agreed, so I called Bruce and asked if it would be all right for me to bring Victor and a couple of his friends over. Bruce said, "Bring them over," which I did that evening.

Bruce brought out the air shield and said in Cantonese, "Peter, show Victor how to hold the shield." Victor was wearing a suit, so he took off his jacket and handed it to me. I asked him about his Rolex, but Victor said it would be all right. I double-checked, "You sure?" Victor replied, "Don't worry." Victor is about 5 feet 7 inches tall and weighs 175 pounds.

I caught a glimpse of Bruce, who had his quintessential smiling glance on his face. He signaled for me to stand behind Victor. We were in the living room and kitchen area. The distance between Victor and the wall was about 20 feet. I set up behind Victor, standing in front of the wall. Bruce asked Victor if he was ready; he nodded his head. Bruce then let loose a side kick and Victor came off the floor and flew right into me. It was exactly like the kick in *Way of the Dragon* (aka *Return of the Dragon*) behind the restaurant where Bruce's real-life family friend and housekeeper Wu Ngan held the shield and Bruce kicked him into the boxes.

Without saying a word, Victor's face expressed total shock and disbelief at what had just transpired. While everyone talked in disbelief, Victor stood up and realized his Rolex was on the floor. I will never forget his expression after that kick. He did not know whether to smile as if everything was all right or to cry.

Don't Think! Feel.

Just like his one-inch punch, one had to feel Bruce's kicks to truly understand his power. There are just a few of us left who have felt his power, and we will never forget. Those who have been kicked or punched by Bruce are among the most fortunate people in the world.

A photographer visited Bruce's home for an article in *Black Belt* magazine. Bruce wanted to demonstrate the power of his side kick, so he asked Ted Wong and me to stand on the other side of the heavy bag with our backs to the bag at separate times. In this way, you would not know when Bruce was going to kick the bag. I could not hear any of Bruce's movements or footwork as he approached the bag, but when he kicked it, the power went right through the bag and hit me in the middle of my back. My head snapped back as if being hit by a car from behind, with my feet coming off the ground and I slammed against the wall. It was fierce and devastating! Bruce's kicks were lethal.

High Kicking Stretching

In earlier years, I understood that Bruce emphasized kicking below the waist. During my training with Bruce, he began working on kicks to the chest and head. One must realize that Bruce was evolving all the time, even with his kicks. He always told me one will always "learn something every day and never stop evolving." I believe that over time, Bruce absorbed what he could from his fellow martial artists like Jhoon Rhee, Chuck Norris, Mike Stone, Joe Lewis, and others. Nonetheless, it always seemed to be when Bruce picked up something from someone, he ended up doing it better than the person he learned it from.

To kick high, Bruce had to increase his flexibility by stretching his legs more thoroughly. At any opportunity, he was constantly stretching, using his pulley rope, or placing his leg on any elevated object in the room. Kicking high or low depends on the situation, and not everyone can kick high effectively, depending on body type and flexibility. And most people's kicks did not have the kind of power that Bruce could deliver: ONE KICK, ONE KILL!

Later, a kicking combination that Bruce liked a lot started with a side kick to the head followed by another side kick to the chest, then a roundhouse slap kick to the face. Bruce used many of these kicks in his movies, which gained him the nickname in Chinese "Lee Three Legs 李三腳" after *The Big Boss* (aka *Fists of Fury*) was released. During that movie, after the jade necklace was ripped off his neck at the ice factory, Bruce's first three kicks against the factory workers earned Bruce that nickname. Bruce was so smooth and quick with his multiple kicks that he appeared to have three legs!

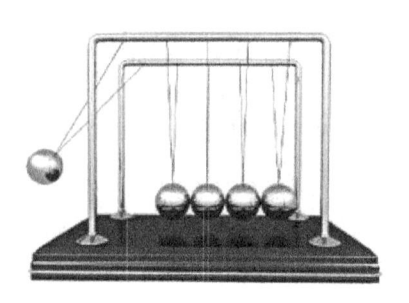

Newton's Cradle

Bruce – High Kick to the Head – Close Range

Practicing high kicks

Peter practices high kicks

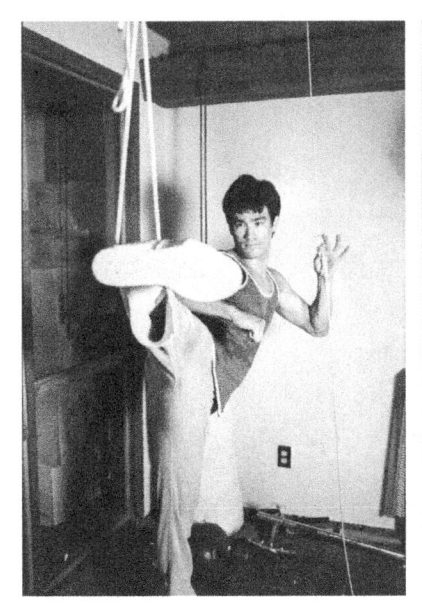

Bruce stretching

6

BRUCE'S BLINDING SPEED AND CAT-LIKE REFLEXES

Bruce was fast. Really fast. Blindingly fast! To be honest, I am unsure what was most impressive about Bruce: his power or his speed. He had incredible power in his kicks and punches, but he was also incredibly fast. I guess it is really a balance of yin and yang — speed and power. For Bruce, you could not have one without the other. To be sure, his physical speed contributed to the power of his kicks and punches.

Bruce told me that speed comes from power, but you also need precision, too. Power, speed, and precision are applied to punching and kicking. To achieve all three is very, very difficult. His movements were explosive and accurate. This is what made his one-inch punch and side kick legendary.

Bruce's close-range hand techniques were a blur. He was exceptional at *pak sao*, stopping his opponent's movements, such as a punch or kick, and coming back with counter-techniques. The best example is from the fight scene in *Way of the Dragon* in which Bruce and Chuck Norris exchange kicks and punches. It was always very simple moves. Bruce was just too powerful and fast. I will even say his techniques were faster than lightning.

The Penny Trick

Bruce often liked to play tricks on people. He would place a penny in their hand. He would tell the person, "Don't let me snatch the penny from the palm of your hand." After a beat, Bruce would ask, "Are you ready?" Then he would try snatching the penny from the person's hand before it closed. When Bruce instructed, "Open your hand," the person would find the penny still there. Bruce would then say, "Let's try it again." He would snatch it again, but this time when the person opened his hand, there would be a nickel in his palm!

Look at his screen test. This is a good representation of how fast Bruce was. Or pay attention to Bruce's interview with Pierre Berton. "You have to put your whole body into it, and you snap it," Bruce said. His punches had snappiness like a whip. When he punches, you can feel the power of his punch through the screen.

Fleet of Foot

Kicking-wise, many people experienced Bruce's kick. When they were asked, "How fast was his kick?" They all said, "If you just blink your eyes, his leg is already by your face." Bruce launched lightning-fast kicks that appeared to come out of nowhere, leaving his opponents stunned and off-balance. This was mentioned by a few fortunate people (or unfortunate people, depending on perspective) who experienced Bruce's kick, usually to the head (Jackie Chan, Sammo Hung, and Wan Kam Leung — Wong Shun Leung's top student). A classic scene was the multiple kicks Bruce delivered to Chuck Norris' head in the highly regarded fight scene at the Colosseum in *Way of the Dragon,* which also contributed to the nickname "Lee Three Legs 李三腳"

Science and Practice of Speed

While it appears that Bruce had a high percentage of fast-twitch muscles, it was not simply his natural abilities. He worked tirelessly to increase his speed with intense physical conditioning and training drills. Through the study of Western fencing, Bruce was able to refine his technique with non-telegraphic motion and explode off the blocks with his superior footwork. Fencing is a highly refined, efficient sport with many strategies and tactics, and Bruce learned a lot about speed and attacking methods from it. As a result, Bruce had a winning combination of theory and practice.

Speed takes on many dimensions. Bruce was a master of them all: initiation, physical, perceptual, mental, and alteration (flow) speed. He also had exceptional reflexes and hand-eye coordination, helping him react quickly against his opponent's attack. This goes beyond the intellectual. Bruce was instinctual, like a cat. He had this innate sense to read his opponent and anticipate the attack.

Bruce assigned us coordination exercises like one hand rubbing the thigh and the other hand in a fist bouncing up and down on the other thigh. Then he would tell us to switch motions between the two hands. This cultivated what is called in Chinese "one mind, two purposes" (一心二用).

Perception — a Lesson in Jeet Kune Do

During one class, Bruce showed me some footwork, and then some front kicks. While we faced each other, Bruce told me to kick him. Every time I raised my leg to kick him, his foot was already in front of my knee. After a few times, I asked him how he did that? Bruce answered, "I can feel your shoulder move; that's how I knew you were starting to kick me." The next morning, I watched myself in front of a mirror at home and slowly moved my leg up. I could not see my shoulder move. I think Bruce could feel it when I advanced on him. He was just too sharp and alert. He could sense the slightest movement of my intention. It was like he could read my mind.

Bruce also told me that when facing your opponent, you can see it in his eyes. One's eyes show a lot, and if one is in great physical condition, one can psych the opponent out. Bruce was very good at knowing when his opponent had a momentary lapse of concentration and was not paying close attention to him and the fight. During this split-second opportunity, Bruce would launch his attack. As a result, he could bridge longer distances and still make his opponent miss.

Feints 虛則實之實則虛之

To penetrate his opponent's defenses, Bruce preferred to use feints before his punching or kicking attack. The opponent would react to Bruce's fake attack, creating an opening to his intended target. It could be misdirection or a change in rhythm. One of Bruce's signature feints was a fake kick to the shin followed immediately by a kick to the head. Bruce also would feint with his hands, but they were too fast; seldom could an opponent perceive them, a case of being felt versus being seen.

Bruce was also a master of broken rhythm and timing. He would lure his opponent into a lackadaisical, mechanical rhythm. Then suddenly, Bruce would zing a punch in between the beats or sometimes slightly hesitate, then deliver a stinging blow or kick.

Breaking Boards (Synthesis of Speed, Power, and Precision)

Although he told the character O'Hara (played by martial artist Bob Wall) in *Enter the Dragon* that "boards don't hit back," Bruce became quite adept at breaking boards, but he did it his way. While many of the karate and *taekwondo* martial artists would have their partner(s) support the board with their outstretched arms so as to make it easy to break, Bruce had the volunteer hold it with one hand or he would even toss the board in the air and break it with a punch or kick as it was coming down. Bruce could do this because of his focused power, speed and precision at the last moment of impact. An interesting point is that punching and kicking a piece of paper hanging from a string helped Bruce hone his board breaking because it helped him perfect his timing and distance. Bruce could break boards with a one-inch punch and five boards with a side kick while his volunteer only held the top of the boards so there was no support.

Catching Quarters

How fast are Bruce's punches? The best way for me to explain this is when I visited Bruce in Hong Kong in 1972. He said he wanted to make a Western movie during the period when the Chinese were working on the railroad. He showed me a book about guns on the cover. He said, "I am starting to practice quick draws." He took out five quarters and placed them along his arm. Then he said, "Watch this." He snapped his arm up, launching the quarters in the air, then caught them as they were falling. He caught all five in his fist. He laughed and asked me if I wanted to try. "Sure!" I said. I placed the five coins on my arm, lining them up a few inches apart. I snapped my arm up to catch the coins while they were falling, and I could only catch one. I insisted, "Wait a minute, let me try it again." I just did not realize how difficult it was. After quite a few attempts, I could only catch three.

In all his movies, Bruce's punches and kicks were so fast that he made it look slow. That is why the audience could see his action stroke by stroke and kick by kick. Even today, no one can produce fight scenes like Bruce's.

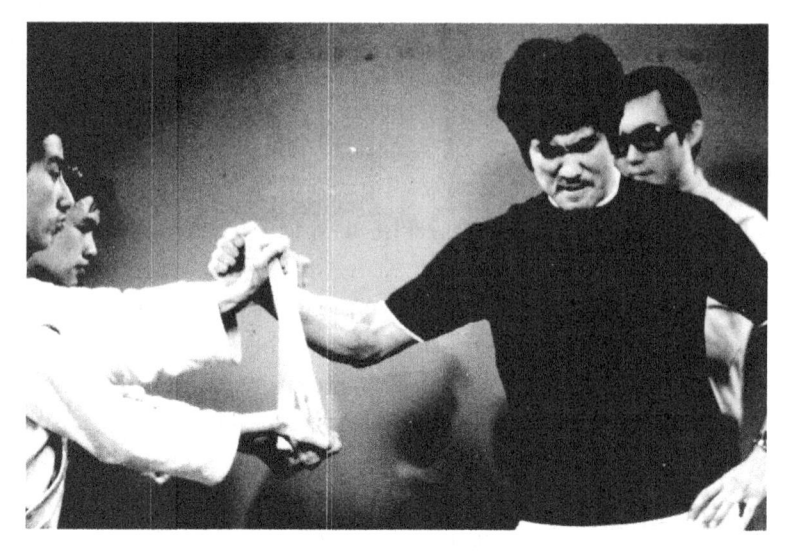

Bruce breaking boards

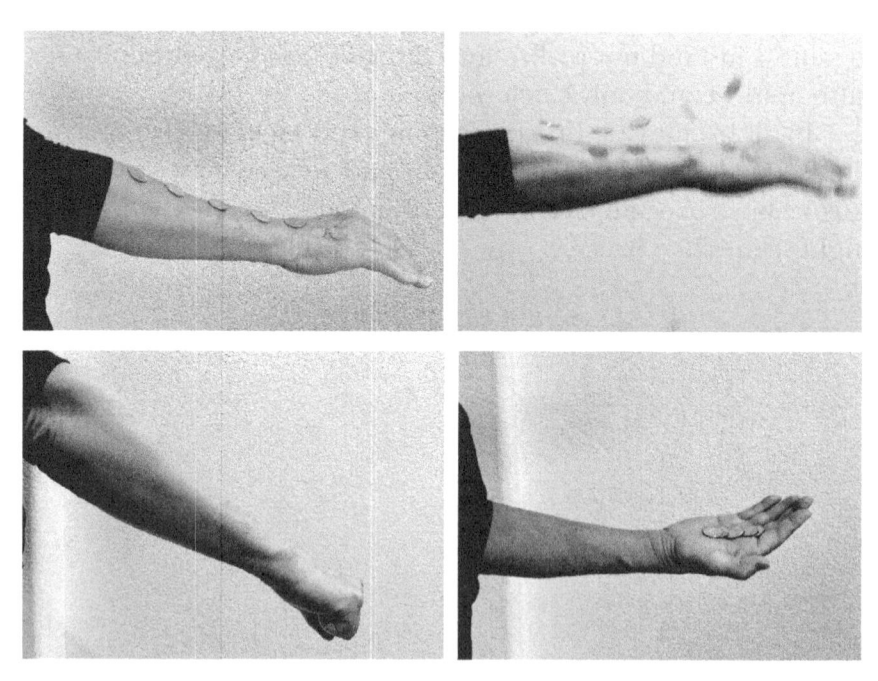

When I was in Hong Kong, Bruce demonstrated catching the five coins.
Try it, then you'll realize how fast Bruce was.

7

AFTER TRAINING – A CLOSE, PERSONAL BOND FORMS

After the training sessions, I realized that my relationship with Bruce was becoming more like a friendship than just being his student. The class was approximately an hour from 7 to 8 p.m., but I always stayed "shooting the bull" until around 11 p.m. to midnight. These are the times when I really miss Bruce, talking with him about how martial arts is a philosophy of life along with a healthy dose of jokes and "locker room talk." We had the same sense of humor, constantly joking. This was also when I would learn the most.

Bruce and I had a lot in common. We would typically converse in Cantonese, our native tongue, then switch to English when Linda showed up. We both grew up in Hong Kong, went to the same school at St. Francis Xavier, and even shared common interests such as dancing, practicing wing chun, and working in show business. I even ended up marrying an American woman.

Bruce was intensely proud of being Chinese. He would say, "Peter, remember even though we live in the USA and are married to American women, deep down inside we are still Chinese." Bruce was very proud of his Chinese heritage and culture, which basically involved gung fu philosophies as "a way of life."

One must understand that Chinese martial arts come from Chinese culture. With martial arts being around for as long as Chinese civilization, there is a lot of culture and morals that have been absorbed in martial arts philosophy. That is why Chinese martial arts are so rich and multilayered, offering more than simply self-defense and health benefits.

With Hong Kong as a British colony in those days, we both understood Eastern and Western ways of culture. Bruce combined the best of both cultures. Because of this understanding, we communicated on a different level. We understood each other without saying a word. We could feel and sense each other; if we both looked at something, we would turn to each other, and both understand.

We also bonded over the renowned Chinese martial arts (wuxia) novels of the 1950s written by Jin Yong that I grew up with in Hong Kong, such as *The Legend of the Condor Heroes*. They had become instant classic martial arts novels, widely regarded among the greatest works of Chinese literature.

A central theme of these novels is the philosophy of martial arts, viewed as a means of self-improvement, both physically and spiritually. Martial arts principles included balance and harmony, softness overcoming hardness, adaptability, perseverance, hard work, ethics, and morality. Practitioners of martial arts strive to perfect their techniques and cultivate their inner strength to better themselves and use their skills and abilities for the greater good. Martial artists adhere to a code of honor and behave with integrity and respect toward others. Loyalty and honor are paramount qualities. They set a high moral standard and instill virtue in martial artists. These ideas have become deeply ingrained in Chinese culture, and they continue to influence the practice and teaching of martial arts to this day.

We also discussed what is known as the Four Great Classical Novels of Chinese literature: 1) *Journey to the West* 西遊記, 2) *Outlaws of the Marsh* 水滸傳, 3) *Romance of the Three Kingdoms* 三國演義 and 4) *Dream of the Red Chamber* 紅樓梦. We loved to talk about these cultural-historical books for hours on end.

Suffice it to say, all these novels were a huge inspiration for impressionable young men like Bruce and me growing up in Hong Kong. They provided Bruce a foundation for excellence in martial arts, so much so that he used some terms from Jin Yong's novels in the fight scene in *Way of the Dragon* behind the restaurant, such as "Movement No. 4 - Dragon Seeks Its Path" and "Dragon Whip Its Tail!" In tribute, the following chapters use terminology from these novels to describe Bruce as a martial artist.

Photos of Chinese Classics of Jin Yong Martial Arts Books

8

FROM LIGHT AS A SWALLOW TO HONEST EXPRESSION

Bruce made kicking look easy and effortless. He was graceful with his footwork. There is a gung fu phrase in Chinese: "身輕如燕 — the body is as light as a swallow." Bruce's movement looked so light, but he contained unbelievable power in his kicks with control and precision. How was he able to achieve such a high degree of devastating power yet make it appear so easy and effortless?

Bruce achieved this through exercise. His No. 1 exercise was jogging — he jogged every day, rain, or shine. This not only enhanced Bruce's stamina but also his swift movement. He would occasionally wear ankle weights when jogging and practicing light kicks. After he removed the weights, his feet appeared to be quicker and lighter, but the power in his kicks remained.

However, I also believe the main reason Bruce was so light and graceful was that he practiced a lot of cha-cha dancing, so much so that he won the cha-cha championship in Hong Kong. Having studied dance myself, I can say that one must be well-coordinated, have a sense of rhythm, and be agile to move quickly, easily, and elegantly to control one's movements. The dancer needs to be aware of his partner and guide his or her movements. Patterns are learned and broken. Doesn't that sound like the qualities needed in martial arts? With Bruce's emphasis on footwork, mobility, and adaptability, one can see all this in his fight scenes.

I recall watching Bruce with amazement when he practiced with the top and bottom bag. It looked like he was dancing with it, punching, and kicking it effortlessly in sync with the bag's movement. Ted Wong could strike it well, but I was terrible with it.

Any highly trained martial artist would understand when they watch Bruce in the movies: He was not a paper tiger. Although his stuntmen reacted to his kicks for fight scenes, Bruce was the real deal. His kicks had to be felt rather than just seen. The reason the movie audience could see each move of Bruce's kicks and punches was because Bruce was so fast that he made it look slow. They also could feel them because of Bruce's realism and emotional intensity in the fighting scenes.

With dancing, there is also a sense of showmanship and expression in the movement, facial expressions, and gracefulness. Ever since he was a child, Bruce was known to be a ham, which was evident in his childhood films in Hong Kong. He coined the phrase "the art of expressing the human body" with martial arts, but I believe this cut across disciplines. From his dancing to his earlier martial arts demonstrations and later to his martial arts films, Bruce was expressing himself.

In the Pierre Berton interview, Bruce attributed his success in the movies because he was "honestly expressing himself." He was real and his honesty was on display on the movie screen. Bruce's fight scenes were the same way — in contrast to the long, sometimes dull fight scenes in Hong Kong martial arts films at the time. Audiences were drawn to Bruce's magnetism and charisma because he was genuine.

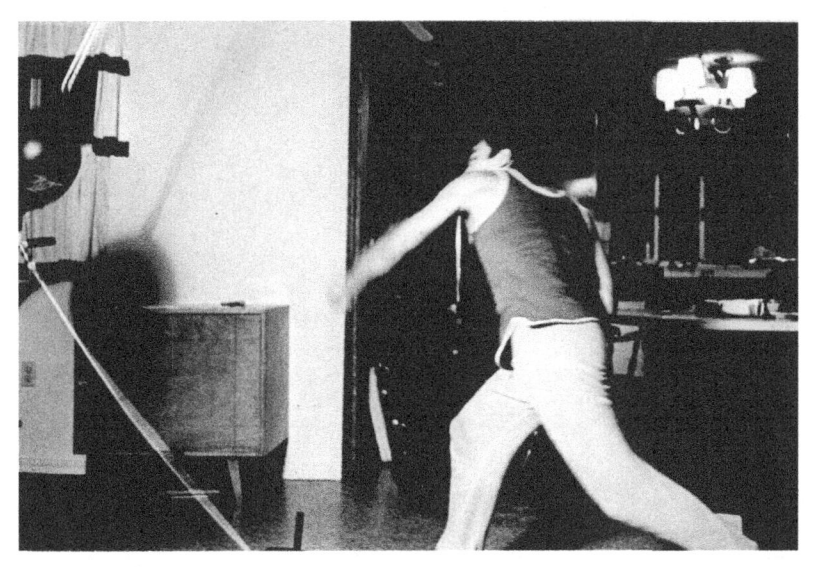

Bruce practices double-end bag, Bruce loves boxing.

9

THE PERFECT MOVE: INTERCEPTING

*If the enemy doesn't move, you don't move.
If the enemy moves, you move first!*
(敵不動己不動,敵一動己先動)

When we sparred in the backyard, I noticed that Bruce would often wait for me to attack him. He then would counter my movement. He was so perceptive at reading me and the timing of my attack. He would respond so quickly with the proper response, intercepting my motion/movement. At the same time, I could hardly read Bruce, much less mount an effective offense to his lack of movement or loss of balance or timing. Bruce was silent, motionless, studying me. He was so still, like a cat, just waiting for me to make a mistake, then pounce! With Bruce, it was like a quick-draw standoff: Despite me drawing first, he had beat me to the punch. 後發先至

When Bruce gave demonstrations, he would instruct his partner to come at him with anything. He would say, "Do not worry. Attack me any way you like, and I will fit in." This made the partner nervous because he would never know what Bruce was going to do or what was coming at him.

One can see some of this in the sparring that Bruce did at the Long Beach tournaments. There is a lot to learn just by watching these clips. Bruce often had his arm extended, sticking out to measure the gap, the distance between him and his opponent. The term "gap" was constantly mentioned when we were training: maintaining the gap, bridging, or closing the gap, etc. It is with the knowledge of the gap that one can intercept an attack or use a broken rhythm to beat the opponent.

Bruce's sense of fighting was so highly tuned that we could sense what the opponent was going to do. Bruce told the young student in *Enter the Dragon*, "Do not think! Feel. ..." It takes a lot of experience to feel the situation, much less see what is going on. Bruce talked a lot about "fitting in" with the opponent, which involves feeling and sensing him.

With this all being said, this principle also upholds the philosophy of gung fu, which is used for self-defense. If your opponent (enemy) is not going to hurt you, then you are not going to hurt him. But if you know he is going to hurt you, then you must hurt him first. 敵不動己不動,敵一動己先動 This virtue is never to be discarded.

10

THE UNITY OF MIND AND BODY 身意合一

In the restored version of *Enter the Dragon*, there is a scene with an elder monk (portrayed by actor Roy Chiao) that follows the initial fight scene with Sammo Hung. This scene was originally cut from the 1973 version but was restored in 1998. It is a revealing scene with Bruce describing the ultimate level in martial arts: "When the opponent expands, I contract. When he contracts, I expand. I do not hit. It hits all by itself." The Chinese phrase 身意合一 *("sun yee hop yut"* — the mind and body as one) refers to the integration of mind and body. You do not think when you face an opponent; you feel. As I mentioned earlier, Bruce used the term "feel" a lot.

I recall Bruce telling me that after learning different styles or techniques, all the techniques that you learned would remain in the back of your head, so when you face the opponent, do not think, or anticipate what the opponent is going to do. You cannot think since you do not know what your opponent is going to do. You must empty your mind and adapt to the situation. With this, one must decrease what one has learned (hacking away the nonessentials), keeping only what is useful and mastering it (that is, practicing a kick 10,000 times). So, the key is you do not move first (gung fu is for self-defense), but if the opponent does attack, you automatically counter it without thinking about which counter to use. It hits all by itself. 身意合一

It hits all by itself.

11

BRUCE LEE: REEL OR REAL FIGHTER

When Bruce was asked, "Are you really that good?"
"If I say I'm good, you will think I am boasting, but if I say I'm not
good, you know I am lying!"
**(Interview with Bruce Lee and Ted Thomas)

After Bruce passed, some prominent martial artists on the competition circuit questioned Bruce's fighting prowess, saying that he was just a martial arts movie star instead of a real fighter, a so-called paper tiger without any fighting experience. I will plainly say that Bruce was the real deal and could wipe up the floor with them.

You must understand that Bruce had plenty of fights in the streets and on the rooftops of Hong Kong in the 1950s, where there were very few rules. Bruce also fought in a boxing competition that he won at St. Francis Xavier. During the fight with Wong Jack Man, Wong wanted to set some rules, but Bruce said, "No, this will be no holds barred!" Bruce did not compete because he had the killer instinct:

> *"Forget about winning and losing; forget about pride and pain. Let*
> *your opponent graze your skin and you smash into his flesh; let him*
> *smash into your flesh and you fracture his bones; let him fracture your*

> *bones and you take his life! Do not be concerned with escaping safely —
> lay your life before him." **(Tao of Jeet Kune Do)*

Bruce trained hard to make it "one kick, one kill; one punch, one kill." Bruce also had a hot temper, which I believe contributed to his life's energy and vitality. His mindset for fighting was to put it all on the line. Make no doubt that Bruce was every bit the fighter that one sees on the screen.

I can understand why some people may believe that Bruce was not formidable because he made it look so easy and graceful. And his good looks and cockiness made it seem like it was all a show. But Bruce was every bit the killer.

People ask me why Bruce did not compete in tournaments. He was so far ahead of the times. He would not subject himself to point fighting or light sparring. We donned boxing gloves, chest protectors, and headgear to go "all out" when sparring. Why do you think that three of the most highly regarded fighters at the time sought out Bruce? He had something no one else had, so they wanted to learn from him and see whether they could achieve the same.

Bruce made it "one kick, one kill". He was every bit the killer.

One punch one kill

12

PHYSICAL CONDITIONING AND JOGGING

"JKD, ultimately, is not a matter of pretty techniques but of highly developed spirituality and physique." **(Tao of Jeet Kune Do)

Let me be perfectly clear: Bruce's success was largely attributed to his perseverance and hard work in his craft. This is clear in his complete dedication to his physical development. Bruce was the pinnacle of fitness. He used to refer to it as scientific training, and Bruce was on the cutting edge of the fitness revolution, training like a modern professional athlete, but more than 60 years ago!

Bruce believed there was too much attention paid to techniques in martial arts and not enough athletic physical training. At that time, traditional stylists thought it was sufficient to repeat basic techniques as their primary form of exercise. Too much time was spent on the development of techniques and too little on the physical development of the individual. As a result, physical training was one of the most neglected factors in many martial arts. Bruce would say, "You do not know what is going to happen to you today when you walk out of your house. Anything can happen. That is the reason why you must keep yourself in shape every day."

It does not matter what style you teach or train in; just add athletic physical training to your curriculum and you will notice the difference in a few short months. Bruce said, "You only have two hands and two legs, you better train every part of your body. When I visited Bruce, I estimated that 30 percent of the time was spent on techniques while 70 percent was on athletic physical training. In many ways, Bruce's training resembled that of a professional prizefighter's workout.

Jogging and the Abdominals

Bruce Lee considered jogging to be the cornerstone of his training regimen, emphasizing its vital role in gung fu. He once advised me, "Peter, if you're truly dedicated to mastering gung fu, you must begin by incorporating jogging into your routine." Curious to learn more, I asked him for guidance on how to proceed. Bruce instructed me to embark on a daily jogging practice, starting with an arduous distance of 25 miles, with the stipulation of sprinting the final half mile. This demanding routine was to be maintained for 30 days, acknowledging that it might require many hours of commitment. However, Bruce stressed that this level of dedication was necessary to truly embrace gung fu.

Following the initial 30-day period, Bruce suggested gradually decreasing the distance over the subsequent three months. The revised plan entailed jogging 20 miles per day for the next 30 days, followed by 15 miles for the subsequent 30 days and further reducing it to 10 miles for the following 30 days. Ultimately, the aim was to settle into a routine of 3 to 5 miles per day, rain, or shine, with a significant emphasis placed on sprinting the last half mile.

Furthermore, once you start this regimen, if you skip a day of jogging, it will result in a setback equivalent to losing the progress of the preceding two days in terms of endurance and stamina. Additionally, he emphasized the need to gradually increase the jogging pace as time progressed.

When I heard that, I knew Bruce was trying to tell me something. Nothing comes easy, even if you have the best teacher in the world. In the end, it all depends on the student's dedication.

Bruce's obsession with jogging stemmed from his fight with Wong Jack Man in Oakland. It was a wake-up call. Before that fight, Bruce thought he was in pretty good shape, but he almost ran out of gas chasing for about three minutes before taking Wong to the floor and making him submit. It really bothered him. Never was he going to be in that situation again. He would train to the maximum and be prepared and ready!

Bruce had an ulterior reason for jogging, too. He would tell me, "When you get into a situation, try your best to get out of it. Only when it is 100 percent necessary and you cannot get out, then you must take care of business with one to three moves. If you cannot make that happen, you better turn around and start running."

Jogging is the best way to give you stamina and endurance, but it is also the best exercise for your abdominal muscles. All your power comes from the core. Bruce believed the abdominals were the most important muscle group for a martial artist because virtually every movement requires some degree of abdominal motion.

Without the power from your core, the power or speed will not be there. While his aerobic capacity might not be so evident, Bruce's abdominals clearly reflected his hard work. Bruce was highly dedicated to training his abs daily, frequently performing sit-ups, crunches, leg raises, v-ups, and Roman chair exercises throughout the day, even while watching TV. Bruce's abs were legendary, even setting the bar high for bodybuilders.

Some good examples of Bruce demonstrating his core strength are in *Enter the Dragon* scenes when he is entering the drug factory by lowering himself down the rope with his legs held horizontal and when O'Hara (played by Bob Wall) enters Bruce's room while Bruce has his leg held up and extended.

Scientific Method

One difference between Bruce's years in Seattle and Oakland to those in Los Angeles is the attention he paid to how athletes train their bodies and fuel them with nutrition. As I reflect on my years with Bruce compared to today's personal trainers, I am amazed at how Bruce trained himself as a true professional athlete. He did extensive research into many physical training books and bodybuilding magazines, then he used a scientific approach with his body as his laboratory.

Today in mixed martial arts, the head coach does not need to know everything. He hires a variety of coaches: strength and conditioning, stand-up fighting, striking, ground fighting, nutrition, etc. But Bruce did it all by himself!

One day in 1968, I met Bruce at his house to accompany him to James Coburn's private lesson. When I arrived at 9 a.m., Bruce was already on his stationary bicycle, drenched with sweat. After a few minutes, he stopped and told me he had been riding for almost an hour.

The stationary bicycle was close to the kitchen. He wiped the sweat off with a towel and went to the kitchen sink where he had a blender. He placed some vegetables and fruit into it. While it blended, Bruce went to the refrigerator, took out a raw egg, and slightly cracked it. He then dropped it in his mouth while looking at me. He asked if I would like to try one to which I shook my head no. I said to myself, "Hmm, interesting. If I try it, I might just vomit."

Then he went back to the blender, poured the juice into a cup, and drank it. He stepped to the table and Linda placed a small plastic bag in front of him. Bruce opened the bag filled with supplements and said he took them every day. I cannot remember every supplement, but I do remember it included vitamin A, vitamin C, vitamin E, and amino acids.

Conditioning the Body

As a blend of Eastern and Western methods, Bruce also did things like toughening the skin on his fists. He would do more than 500 repetitions punching the sandbag on a given day. One day, he went out to the front of his house and broke a brick with his fist. That is when Bruce realized, "Mind over matter," and I noticed he didn't do much with the sandbag anymore and shifted his attention to weights.

Bruce also worked with the wing chun wooden dummy to condition his forearms. Striking the wooden arms of the training apparatus toughened up Bruce's forearms. This came in handy when boxing because Bruce used the "blades" of his forearms to cut into his opponent's arm muscles when intercepting the opponent's punches. Although his hands were gloved up, his unpadded forearms were exposed and dug into his opponent's arms. Bruce's countermoves were also offensive.

Strength Training with Weights

By the time I started training with Bruce, he was really into weight training. There was a widespread view, even by professional football players in the 1960s, that weightlifting was considered detrimental and even dangerous. Many professional football teams banned it. But Bruce recognized that strength and conditioning were crucial to becoming the ultimate fighter. By lifting weights and performing isometric exercises, Bruce increased his strength immensely, which also helped improve his speed.

In addition, Bruce transformed his body into one of the fittest bodies in the history of athleticism. Bruce learned a lot from Oakland students James Lee and Allen Joe, who was a bodybuilding champion and a contemporary of Jack LaLanne.

Pushing Out 65 Pounds

One night before class, Bruce told Ted and me to watch him. He picked up a 65-pound barbell to his chest, then pushed it straight out from his chest and held it for about 10 seconds before he put it down. Bruce then turned to us and said, "Come try it." I went first and lifted the barbell to my chest. When I tried to push it out, I realized, "Wow, no way!" Right away, I set the barbell down to the floor and Bruce had that smile on his face. Ted went next, picking up the barbell to his chest and trying to push it straight out and the same thing happened. Like me, he had to let the barbell go down and shook his head in disbelief. We could not hold it for even a split second!

Bruce said, "Let me try something else," placing more weight on the bar. I asked how much weight now, and Bruce answered 135 pounds. With one hand, Bruce lifted the whole 135 pounds up in the air. Ted and I were shocked. "Wow! How is that possible?" I asked myself. Bruce only weighed 135 pounds at the time, and with one hand, he lifted his whole-body weight.

Grip Strength

Another important thing Bruce always worked on was his grip. In the early years, Bruce had a special weight machine that Oakland student George Lee built for him to increase his grip strength and build his forearms. Bruce had to squeeze the bars of the machine with his fingers to "lift the weight." However, with this device, Bruce could not close his hand to clench it into a tight fist. In later years, Bruce constantly practiced his grip by squeezing a small item like a floatable foam sponge keychain. In this way, it was not the amount of weight but rather the repetition and closing his hand completely into a tightly clenched fist, unlike other equipment. Bruce kept it with him all the time and used it whenever he could.

A large part of Bruce's success was because of the time he put into himself. I remember seeing the Marcy machine with all its apparatuses for multiple exercises in Bruce's living room of his home in Hong Kong. He was constantly looking for ways to improve himself. He put in long hours every day to make himself the greatest martial artist that ever lived. Today, all the equipment for physical training is amazing. I could only imagine what Bruce could have contributed if he were alive today.

Bruce is jogging.

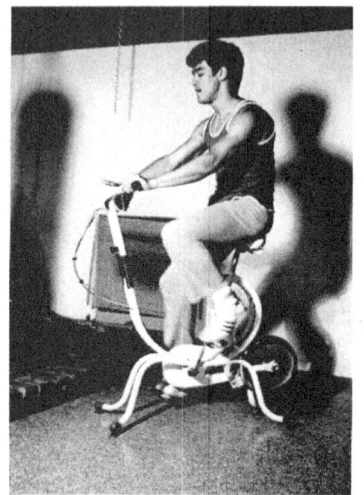

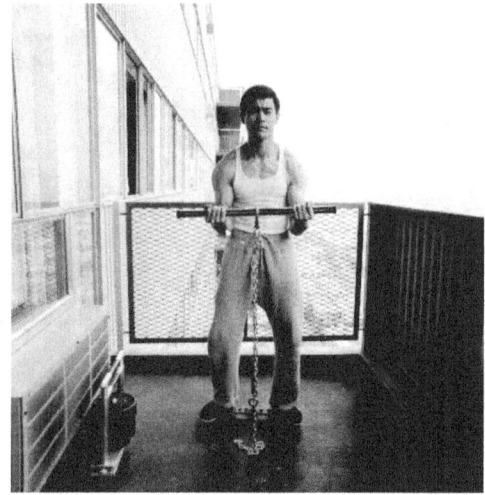

Cycling and isometric workouts.

Weightlifting

Bruce used a scientific approach with his body as his laboratory.

13

BRUCE'S BACK INJURY

With Bruce being his own trainer, it would not surprise today's top experts if he injured his back. Bruce was his own coach; he did not have any spotters. His drive probably caused him to overtrain and not give his body enough time to recover. Bruce pushed himself to the maximum!

I called Bruce about coming to class, but he had to cancel the Wednesday class until further notice. I asked what happened, and he said he hurt his back by doing a "good morning" exercise before warming up properly as he usually did. The good-morning exercise involves placing a barbell on your shoulders and bending over at the waist, keeping your legs straight.

I told him that I would be checking in and to please let me know if there was anything I could do for him. It was a sad period when the classes were canceled due to his injury. I would call Bruce once or twice a week to see how he was feeling. This was a rough period for Bruce. He suffered financially, and Linda had to get a job. This was a blow to Bruce because, in those days, Chinese culture expected the husband to take care of his family.

With classes canceled, I moved to Las Vegas to help my uncle, who owned a custom tailor clothing business named John Lieu Original on Las Vegas Boulevard, next to the Sands Hotel and Casino. My uncle was famous for designing wardrobes for many top celebrities of that time: Paul Anka, Ike and Tina Turner, Siegfried and Roy, Kenny Rogers, and many of the showrooms' maître d's, captains, and casino executives. During that period, I learned about the importance of the fabric selected. The fabric is essential based on the way it feels and lays, and its quality is crucial to achieving an elegant, lavish, and luxurious appearance.

I stayed with my uncle for about three months. When Bruce improved, he resumed classes and I immediately returned to Los Angeles. I mentioned to Bruce that I was working for my uncle in his tailored clothing business. I offered to measure him so that my uncle could make a pair of custom pants for Bruce. As I recall, they were made of dark material and had a slight bell bottom. Bruce appreciated first-class quality.

14

BRUCE AS A TEACHER

While I am not sure if Bruce's other students addressed him as *sifu*, after a couple of classes, I decided to address Bruce in Cantonese as *dai sifu* (大師傅) a teacher at the highest level. It sounded inappropriate at the time, but Bruce knew exactly what I meant. I just could not address him as sifu because he was extraordinary and deserved more than just the term sifu. He was above all of that. He was the founder of jeet june do.

When it came to teaching, Bruce's patience was limited. He expected you to pick up quickly what he was showing you. He would explain the reason for the move in detail, and after Bruce finished, I could not explain it the same way that he had just a few minutes before. Simply, Bruce was a genius among us normal, average human beings.

I recall Bruce asking me, "What is a hamburger?" He would go into detail about the step-by-step process of making a hamburger: Ground the beef, get some lettuce, and take a few lettuce leaves, get a tomato and cut a couple of slices, take one slice of onion, and slightly toast your hamburger bun. Add mayo, ketchup, and mustard, and grill the beef while placing the tomato, lettuce, and onion on the bun. When the patty is done, place it on the bun. As clear as he made the detailed instructions, after a few seconds, I could not repeat all the steps.

Bruce also had an unusual talent to evaluate. After talking with you a few times or having you perform a few moves, he knew exactly what to do with you. He would know you better than you know yourself. Bruce could have been a great politician because he never gave you a direct answer. And his way was not to offend anyone when giving the answer. This way, Bruce could charm people. He could make you feel good and at the same time help you save face.

Sparring with Bruce

During this period, Bruce used to say that a lot of dryland swimming was taught with martial arts. He meant that there was too much attention paid to forms/*kata* and not enough to full-contact sparring. To really learn how to fight, as if one wants to learn how to swim, one must jump into the pool by sparring with newfound techniques and training against the opponent.

Bruce recognized that a student quickly learns what works when sparring. As a result, the student begins to simplify his arsenal. No longer is there a need for more techniques or an accumulation of them but rather the correct use of them. It is better for one to devote the needed hours of practice to simple and effective techniques for their correct execution and timing. It is not how much one learns but how much one absorbs and applies. The best techniques are the simple ones executed correctly.

In terms of my personal experience, when sparring, I noticed that Bruce concentrated on boxing with Ted and kicking with me. I gathered this was to test Bruce to spar against his opponent's best techniques but also to give the student a level of confidence.

Quality, not Quantity

Bruce was more concerned about quality than quantity, and that was the reason he closed the Los Angeles school. That is a direct quote from Bruce himself. Once he realized all students were different, he knew he could not mass-produce quality martial arts students. They all had different needs and required personal attention. I recall Bruce mentioning having different techniques for different people. No one has the same physique, and everyone's background is different.

However, one's character was the most important attribute for Bruce. He did not care where you came from, your race, rich or poor, if your character was honorable. Bruce believed that a person's character defined his or her true worth with integrity, discipline, and a commitment to personal growth. Earlier, Bruce even turned down the idea of franchising schools after the discontinuation of *The Green Hornet* because he did not want to prostitute his art even though he was low on money. Bruce was a man of principle.

Bruce sparring demonstration in one of Long Beach's demonstrations.

15

BRUCE'S INTELLIGENCE AND PHOTOGRAPHIC MEMORY

Bruce had a library containing about 2,500 books, mostly related to all kinds of systems of gung fu and martial arts, boxing, fencing, Eastern and Western philosophy, and most important, athletic training. He read so many books; the list went on and on. We know he read them since there are annotations in nearly every book.

Let us assume Bruce read his 2,500 books from 1959 to 1973: Fourteen years equate to 15 books a month or about a book every two days. Many successful people recommend reading one book a month because it increases knowledge and understanding, improves thinking and cognitive functioning, and enhances empathy and understanding of different perspectives and cultures. It allows the exploration of new ideas, and different worlds, and connecting with others.

Bruce's Three Key Ingredients:

1. Photographic memory (**過木不忘**)
2. Knowing the body (anatomy)
3. Taking care of your temple (nutrition's)

Bruce had possessed all this talent himself. He had a photographic memory and accumulated knowledge through reading books. When someone showed him a certain move, Bruce could quickly pick it up and improve it, even better than the person who showed it to him. This was the case with the *nunchaku* from Dan Inosanto, kicking from Jhoon Rhee or Chuck Norris, or bodybuilding from Allen Joe. Bruce was basically a self-made man.

Something that really impressed me about Bruce was his knowledge of human anatomy. He knew every bone and muscle in the body.

Bruce really worked at what made it better through all his research. Bruce combined Eastern and Western cultures and different martial arts around the world, synthesizing the knowledge together with what he learned from real life. With his deep understanding of gung fu, he found it to be a philosophy of life.

It is important to revisit the Pierre Berton BBC interview, especially when Bruce said, "Martial arts has a very deep, deep meaning as my life is concerned. As an actor, as a martial artist, as a human being, all these I have learned from martial arts."

With his deep understanding of gung fu,
he found it to be a philosophy of life.

16

JEET KUNE DO — THE ENIGMA

Truthfully, I do not understand why there has been so much controversy about jeet kune do over the years. Bruce was very clear about it. How could his disciples turn JKD into such a mess? Bruce was jeet kune do. Without him, it would have never been relevant. You need to have Bruce Lee, an iconoclast, burn a trail that no one else could.

If Bruce were alive today, he would be like a volcano exploding over what happened to his art. At the same time, if he were here, none of this would be happening. Throughout the world today, there are more countries teaching under JKD's umbrella yet are teaching things that Bruce would never have done, basically ignoring Bruce's teachings. Bruce showed them the way, taking them out of the box, yet they went right back into it.

As for JKD, the only people who can stake a claim are those who received a certificate from Bruce stating they were "personally taught by Bruce Lee." This does not make me an original JKD; I am one of Bruce Lee's original students only and not JKD. I know this sounds confusing, but that is my belief. I was one of the luckiest people to have had the chance to learn from Bruce directly and be along for the ride during Bruce's journey. It was one of the most wonderful, precious times of my life. But I am the first to admit that I am not an expert in JKD.

Jeet Kune Do Is Just a Name

At the end of the day, jeet kune do is just a name. Bruce had made it clear when he created the term in Los Angeles. Yet as of this writing, it is very hard to get away from the term. The reason that JKD is still popular today is because people are capitalizing on Bruce's celebrity. As the saying goes, "There's no business-like show business."

His intention was not just to promote martial arts but also to promote it as a way of life because different styles separate people. Different martial artists will say, "I am better than you." They are always competing against one another to prove, "My technique is better than your technique." So, there is always a lot of conflict, a lot of disagreement. In my opinion, instead of talking, just step into the ring and whoever walks out has the bragging rights.

Ultimately, Bruce regretted naming his art. He feared his followers would misinterpret his way as the only way to truth in martial arts. He said, "If people say that jeet kune do is different from 'this' or 'that,' then let the name jeet kune do be wiped out, for that is what it is, just a name." **(*Tao of Jeet Kune Do*)

Out-of-the-Box Thinking

Bruce explained to me that the easiest way to understand JKD is if one learns more than one style of martial arts, one is "out of the box" and automatically becomes JKD. Traditionally, if you study Shaolin, you must stay with Shaolin. If you study karate, you must stay with karate, etc. Bruce changed this thousands-year-old tradition and urged his students to transcend style, using "no way" as the way. Simple, direct, and nonclassical. Today, I believe many more martial artists throughout the world are, in a way, more like JKD because they are more open-minded than in the past. However, this does not mean that Shaolin or karate are JKD. Rather, the individual is given the freedom to explore.

Unfortunately, even today many jeet kune do practitioners use Bruce Lee's name to promote something. This is a double-edged sword. First, anyone other than the Lee family who attempts to capitalize off Bruce's name or image is immoral and unethical. Even worse is passing off teachings or philosophies as JKD that Bruce had nothing to do with. Some responded by claiming to teach the original JKD. But does this create a box that confines a student's individual growth? And if they evolve, are they no longer original?

It is well-established that the fight with Wong Jack Man in Oakland was a turning point for Bruce. He believed for some time that wing chun was missing something, and that fight confirmed it: wing chun was only effective in close quarters. It does not mean that wing chun is no good, just that it has limitations and Bruce chose to be outside of its confines. In a similar way, Bruce discovered his own personal limitations regarding his stamina, leading him to quadruple his efforts of intense physical training, a rather new approach in classical martial arts. That is what I really want to emphasize to the current JKD practitioners and all martial artists: Pay more attention to athletic physical training.

One must absorb what is useful and discard the rest. I try to share what I learned from Bruce with those who are interested, but they eventually must think out of the box and find their own way. Bruce believed one can learn something every day and evolve. If one is not willing to evolve, how can one improve? And remember, Bruce's philosophies can apply to any path that one chooses, not necessarily just in martial arts. I used it in my business. Just a few simple basic philosophies can go a long way.

We Are All Different

JKD was Bruce's very personal evolution, expression, and philosophy in the martial arts. This meant that Bruce combined Eastern and Western philosophy and culture, scientific training, and his martial arts techniques. Jeet kune do was tailor-made for Bruce since the training and techniques that he honed were for him, which included the physicality of training, the science of biomechanics, and the psychology of human nature to create his own expression in jeet kune do. Unless one has the same body type, movement, mentality, dedication, and resolve as Bruce, then I do not expect anyone who is following the precepts of JKD to resemble Bruce.

It is very important to understand that all of Bruce's students are different. The best way to describe it is to raise your hand and look at your fingers — they are all different. The same was true for each of Bruce's students. They all had different backgrounds, experiences, and opinions. Some studied judo, karate, boxing, *tai chi*, and so on before they trained with Bruce. Some could pick up the training and knowledge faster, some slower. Their cultures and family backgrounds were different, as were their physiques — some tall, some short. Every student is different, so JKD will be different for each person. It does not matter where you are from.

Most of all, Bruce wanted everyone to be themselves — learning and absorbing what works for each and discarding what is useless. Bruce established some basic concepts, but they could change and evolve depending on the student and which period one studied with Bruce. Studying with Bruce in 1964 would be different from studying with him in 1965 and 1965 would be different from 1966 and so on. This can be applied to one's daily life or profession, whether you are working for someone or self-employed. Once you understand the philosophy, you can apply it to your daily life.

Be Water

"Empty your mind.
Be formless, shapeless, like water.
You put water into a cup, it becomes the cup.
You put water into a bottle, it becomes the bottle.
You put it into a teapot, it becomes the teapot.
Now water can flow, or it can crash.
Be water, my friend."
**(Bruce Lee, Pierre Berton Interview and Longstreet)

What did Bruce mean when he said, "Be water?" We all know what it means for one to adapt to the situation, but it takes a while to really understand. It is easy to say, but the meaning is deeper than one realizes. And it can change every minute of a lifetime. It might mean something different a few months or a year from now. One's life keeps evolving, and knowledge and common sense keep evolving. Thus, one's adaptability will change over time.

It changes the way you think. In other words, "be water" is simple, yet over the years, and depending on what one has been through in life, one will understand oneself and truly express oneself.

JKD is a lot like music. People create music. There are only seven musical notes on a chromatic scale, but people use the scale in so many ways and create so many different musical styles and songs. After learning all the different notes, styles, and techniques, Bruce was able to stick with those basic notes and returned to his original freedom of simplicity. Bruce kept his gung fu "way of life" simple.

Evolving

Today, I am afraid many JKD may be "back in the box" by spending too much time on techniques while neglecting the most important part, which is physical training. Instructors just talk about technique. There are so many techniques that I cannot even keep track. JKD's goal is to simplify and not to be complicated. I believe that currently, JKD has gone backward instead of evolving forward. It is my wish that everyone remembers Bruce's philosophy to keep evolving and growing. We must continue to have "no way" as the way and "no style" as the style, meaning all styles as the style, having no limitation. And most important, include daily physical conditioning.

At the end of the day, jeet kune do is just a name.

Bruce showed them the way, taking them out of the box, yet they went right back into it.

All the instructors talk about is technique. There are so many techniques that I cannot even keep track.

Jeet Kune Do: Simply Not a New Style

Bruce made it perfectly clear that he did not create a new style, since that would just create another segment of totality, continuing to restrict one to a single way of doing something, and therefore, limiting one's capacity. Defining JKD, simply as Bruce Lee's style of fighting completely loses its message:", I never wanted to give a name to the kind of Chinese kung fu that I have invented, but for convenience's sake, I still call it Jeet Kune Do. However, I want to emphasize that there is no clear line of distinction between Jeet Kune Do and any other kind of Gung Fu for I strongly object to formality, and to the idea of distinction of branches." - *The Evolution of A Martial Artist

17

MARTIAL ARTS PHILOSOPHY FOR LIFE

"Martial arts have a very deep, deep meaning as my life is concerned, as an actor, as a martial artist, as a human being, all these I have learned from martial arts."
— Bruce Lee, Pierre Berton interview

To truly understand JKD, we must start with what is Chinese gung fu? Very plainly, the first purpose is for health and the second is for self-defense. Once you understand this, then it is easy to understand what Bruce accomplished: He showed the world the importance of physical training and the beauty of martial arts. Basically, gung fu is a way of life. When people begin to understand the Chinese gung fu philosophy, they will have a very different view of it.

Even 50 years after his passing, Bruce Lee is iconic, especially on social media. He is still popular today and will be for many centuries to come around the globe. This is because of his philosophy, his charisma, and his ingenuity. Bruce's goal in life was to show the whole world what gung fu really is — to bring people together, not only as martial artists but also as human beings. Bruce was a humanitarian.

One night after a class, Bruce said to me, "The ultimate martial artist doesn't need to fight or prove anything." He then reminds me of the Chinese saying, "If you have the precious sword, it does not need to be drawn to show people." (有寶劍不用拔出來示人) The premier martial artist is confident of his fighting abilities and remains humble.

As I mentioned earlier, for Bruce, a person's ethics and integrity were extremely important to one's character. For me, jeet kune do is a way of life with the most important thing being about the character and integrity of the individual human being. I guess you could call this martial arts ethics. The Wu Ethics (武德), *Wu De* (gung fu — ethics), is based on social justice and fairness, the oldest moral concepts of mankind. Martial arts are about your word.

One night when Bruce and I were talking, Bruce asked, "Do you know how to improve yourself?" I shook my head and he said, "There is always something good and bad about a person. It is up to you to pick up what is good about this person and forget about the bad, and that is how you improve yourself."

Bruce's Personal Philosophical Lessons

The teachings and philosophies I learned from Bruce and martial arts have been applied to my daily life and my business. It is my desire to express some of Bruce's teachings and what they mean. That is important since Bruce bridged the gap between his original Chinese culture and Western ways of thinking.

Here are some philosophical thoughts Bruce talked to me about after class. He made it very simple when he mentioned them to me, simpler than those he wrote in his notebooks, but the meaning behind them is so strong that I still use them to this day.

Making a mistake or lying — You need to clear it up as soon as possible. Bruce told me to never lie, but if I do, I need to make amends as soon as possible. There is a Chinese saying, "The wok, sooner or later, will have a hole." In other words, if you lie, someday it will eventually come out; it is just a matter of time. Therefore, if you make a mistake, admit it, mend it, accept the consequences, and walk on. No one is perfect.

Two heads are better than one — Bruce often said this phrase, and it has really helped me throughout my life, personally and in business. When you have questions about anything, don't be afraid to ask. If you don't know something, don't hesitate to ask, don't waste time. Before the advent of internet mapping, people would hesitate to stop at a gas station to ask for directions. Don't feel embarrassed that you don't know. Two heads are always better than one.

Swearing — I never heard Bruce swear or speak ill of anyone. Too much time and energy wasted.

Money — When I asked Bruce if money can make one happy, he answered, "I'd rather be miserable with money than miserable without money."

Religion — St. Francis Xavier College is a Catholic school in Hong Kong that Bruce and I both attended. I was baptized as a Catholic. One day, I asked Bruce, "What about God?" Bruce turned to me and said, "God helps those who help themselves. So, who's God!?"

Give credit where it is due — Bruce always gave credit to those he learned something from. Bruce gave credit to Dan Inosanto for introducing the nunchaku to him, Jhoon Rhee and Chuck Norris for showing him some kicks, and Robert Clouse for suggesting the mirror room in *Enter the Dragon*. He mentioned the mirror room in the final fight scene to me when we were talking on the phone.

Happiness — Bruce would say that the most important thing in life is to be happy and that if you find a career that you enjoy doing, and if you do it well, you will eventually be rewarded. Bruce made me happy every time I met him. He always made me laugh; we had a great time together. How do you know you are happy? Bruce would answer, "When you made someone else happy."

Walk On — *If you have a problem – if there is a solution, why worry about it, and if there is no solution why worry about it?*

Bruce's Two Goals in Life

Bruce told me that he only has two goals in life:

1. "To show the world what Chinese gung fu really is" (professional goal)
2. "Take good care of my family" (personal goal)

Nothing mattered more to Bruce than his family (Linda, Brandon, and Shannon). According to our shared Chinese culture, it is the husband's responsibility to take care of his wife and children and provide for them.

What Bruce Did for the Chinese

I had the opportunity to meet the abbot of the Shaolin Temple in 1994 in Beijing. I asked him what he thought of Bruce Lee. He said, "Peter, I said it two times already during a live CCTV interview regarding Bruce Lee. I said Bruce Lee put China back on the map." Being Chinese myself and knowing the abbot's position, I felt honored and happy for Bruce, since I was right ever since the Long Beach tournament that Bruce would make history.

> *Under the sky, under the heavens, there is but one family. It just so happens that people are different.* **(Pierre Berton Show)

Bruce experienced discrimination during his lifetime. As a child, Hong Kong was invaded by the Japanese and under occupation during World War II. After the war, Hong Kong was a colony controlled by the British. In both instances, the Chinese were treated poorly. Bruce's Eurasian bloodline was used against him by some senior wing chun students who convinced the traditional Yip Man to not teach him since Bruce was not 100 percent Chinese. That opened the door, though, for Bruce to continue his studies with Wong Shun Leung, whose practical approach to martial arts put Bruce on his path. When he arrived in Hollywood, acting roles were hard to come by, so Bruce had to go to Hong Kong to prove his worth before an American studio would be interested in giving him a leading role.

Nevertheless, Bruce wanted to unite people, and he was going to do this through the beauty of martial arts. The universal nature of martial arts and its philosophy allowed Bruce to use martial arts to bring people together; it does not matter which country you are from or what race you are.

It is essential to recognize the yin-and-yang aspect of the above phrase: While we are all from the human race, we acknowledge that we are all different, not only physically. We come from different backgrounds, different cultures, different countries, different philosophies. Despite these differences, we are all human, which gives us hope that we can unite. To use only the first half of the phrase is incomplete. You must have one to have the other. It was Bruce's intention that we should work together peacefully. Bruce aimed to unite people through our shared humanity.

Self-Help

First, I would like to explain what the term "study" (學習) means in Chinese. 學 means learning, 習 means practice. It is like going to school. One goes to school every day and learns in class. However, when you go home and do not do the homework, then you are not really absorbing what you learned. In the same way, if you are attending a martial arts class and not practicing what your sifu taught you, what are you accomplishing? One must practice to genuinely learn. What you put in is what you are going to get out.

In the end, it is about self-help. Pay more attention to the training after the class. It is what you put in after school that's more important. The teacher can only show you the way. The rest depends on you. Bruce could only show us the way as a pointer to the truth; we must apply. The results will be different for each student.

Bruce perfectly embodies the practice of self-help. He put in an incredible amount of effort to achieve what he achieved, both with physical training and training his mind. Bruce applied this not only to martial arts but also to making movies. For example, he studied filmmaking and photography. As a result, for *Way of the Dragon,* he did not just act in the film, but he also produced, wrote the script, choreographed the fights, and directed the movie.

More broadly, life itself is your teacher and you are always constantly learning. When one takes responsibility for one's life, one becomes self-reliant and self-sufficient. Then self-knowledge is attained. At the end of the day, it all boils down to Bruce's keyword — self-help. What you put in is what you are going to get out.

Peter and the Abbot of Shaolin Temple 1994.

18

HANGING AROUND WITH BRUCE IN HOLLYWOOD

During the years I knew Bruce in Los Angeles, it was fun and fascinating hanging around with him. I recall karate champions Chuck Norris, Joe Lewis, and Mike Stone visiting for lessons. During a Wednesday class, Bruce was showing Chuck how to do chi sao and I practiced with him while Bruce explained its purpose. They all seemed intensely interested in Bruce and his martial arts.

Bruce put my Screen Extras Guild card to work by having me as an extra on *The Wrecking Crew*, starring Dean Martin (as secret agent Matt Helm), Nancy Kwan, and Sharon Tate. Bruce was the fight choreographer for the film. Mike Stone was the stunt double for Dean Martin, and Chuck Norris and I were henchmen.

Mito Uyehara, the publisher of *Black Belt* magazine, would stop by occasionally. He had studied *aikido* from Koichi Tohei, and besides promoting Bruce in the magazine, he taught Bruce a few techniques in aikido, which Bruce frequently used on me.

In fact, it was Mito who introduced Bruce to Kareem Abdul-Jabbar. I met Kareem once with Bruce to have Chinese food in Chinatown. I remember he ordered shrimp fried rice and drove a Chevrolet Malibu with no back seats. His driver's seat was pushed all the way back. Kareem is really tall, and Bruce and I only reached his waist, but he was a very gentle and quiet person.

The most important thing that Bruce cared about was his hair. Jay Sebring was a famous men's hair stylist known for the "short hair with a long look" cut. Sebring was the coiffeur to many Hollywood stars. He was the person who suggested Bruce to *The Green Hornet* producers for the role of Kato. Tragically, Sebring was killed during the Sharon Tate murders by members of the Charles Manson family. One of Sebring's top students and well-respected hair stylist in his own respect, "Little Joe" Torrenucva, continued to style Bruce's hair.

I first met Steve McQueen with Bruce at Steve's home sometime in 1968. Bruce was to have a class with Steve, so I went with Bruce as the bagman. The house was on top of a hill. At the bottom, there was a gate that had a microphone. Bruce hit the button, announced his name and the gate opened, and we drove up to the hill on the winding road to the top. We entered the stone house, and Steve was in the kitchen. I remember Steve talking about buying a ranch in New Zealand. Unfortunately, there was a change of schedule and Steve could not take the class, so after a short visit, Bruce and I left.

On another occasion, Steve took Bruce and me to see Jean Harlow's former home, which contained a curtain that automatically opened. I cannot remember if someone was interested in purchasing it, but I certainly recall those curtains.

On one of Bruce's birthdays, I was at Bruce's Bel Air home with Ted and Herb when Linda said, "Bruce, Steve is on the phone." Bruce took the call, and when he came back, he told us it was Steve. He was in Palm Springs and was coming to join the class. He had just bought a new car and said he would be at Bruce's in one hour. Ted and I looked at each other astonished. Palm Springs is more than 100 miles away and he can be here in an hour? Well, around an hour later, Steve walked into the house. He showed us his new car: a Porsche with the latest, hottest color for Porsche at the time — racing green. I am sure this is what motivated Bruce to buy his own Porsche.

After class Ted and Herb left, as usual I stayed around and Steve said to Bruce: "Let us go to The Candy Store. Jay Sebring is there already." The Candy Store was an exclusive members-only celebrities' disco in Beverly Hills. When we arrived, there was the usual line of people waiting outside to get in. We walked in with no problem because the security knew Steve. Steve said hello to a lot of people that night, and after a while, Bruce said let us get out of here and I agreed. We did not stay long since it was not Bruce's cup of tea. He did not enjoy socializing, especially in public places, and he did not drink or smoke. Bruce never liked the nightlife and big crowds of people he did not know. That was the last time I saw Steve until the funeral in Seattle.

Bruce would usually bring someone with him while teaching his celebrity private classes when they could not come to his house. In some ways, I was Bruce's sidekick for these private lessons with the celebrities. I believe Ted was one, as well. During these lessons, Bruce needed someone to hold the air shield or focus mitts so he could watch the students perform punches and kicks. Likewise, the student could watch Bruce punch or kick with me holding the equipment to emulate him.

One day, I went with Bruce to James Coburn's house in Beverly Hills. The interior was decorated with a Moroccan theme and different kinds of rugs hung on the walls. It felt like we were in a harem. The smell of incense permeated throughout. James showed Bruce some antiques he had just acquired. Then we went out to the backyard for Bruce to show James how to side-kick with me holding the kicking shield.

After the lesson, Bruce asked me if I could smell the cologne James had on. I said yes and that it smelled terrific, thinking it was something like sandalwood. Bruce said, "A few of the celebrities all like that cologne. I first smelled it on Sharon Tate." Bruce asked me if I would like to have some, to which I said sure. It turned out to be patchouli oil.

Bruce and I headed over to a store on Melrose where James said we could get some of the Moroccan casual clothing he showed us. They turned out to be the kaftans that Bruce and Linda wore in many pictures. I also picked up one for myself. The store also had the cologne James wore — patchouli oil. I like the smell even today.

In late 1968, I went to see Stirling Silliphant with Bruce at his house. Stirling was working on the *Longstreet* script, and he did not want to leave his home, but he wanted a workout. When we walked into his house, we went directly to the garage and Bruce started to practice some sparring with Stirling and later had him do some sidekicks on the shield I held.

After a while, Stirling was sweating heavily, his sweatshirt drenched. An hour had passed when Bruce and Stirling went into his study while I waited in the living room. Bruce came out of Stirling's study, and we left. On the road, Bruce told me that Stirling was creating a script for him to act in the *Longstreet* TV show and that he would create a small part for him in the movie *Marlowe*.

Sure enough, Stirling did write a small but memorable role for Bruce in *Marlowe*. I remember Bruce rehearsing his lines at his home, placing five $100 bills on his desk. The original script called for Bruce's character to be killed by the star of the film portrayed by James Garner. But Bruce never let anyone kill him in the movies because they simply could not for real. Stirling rewrote the script where Bruce misses Garner with his flying kick and flies off the rooftop, dying in spectacular style. Bruce was excited to get a new suit for the role from the Brioni clothing store on the Sunset Strip. To be honest, he was more excited about the Brioni suit than he was about the part! Bruce was a classy dresser, and he appreciated quality.

To be honest, he was more excited about the
Brioni suit than he was about the part.

Bruce Lee in Marlowe

Bruce and Stirling Silliphant

Bruce and Steve McQueen

Bruce with Steve James Coburn

Bruce with Kareem Abdul Jabbar

The kaftan from a store on Melrose Road Los Angeles

19

BRUCE'S CHARISMA, MAGNETISM AND HUMOR

There was something about Bruce. He was charismatic and had a magnetic personality. He could walk into a room where there were a lot of people, and after talking for only a few minutes, people would automatically be drawn to him. Bruce would be the center of attention, entertaining the whole party. Whenever he was with a group of people, he would be the only person talking and you could tell everyone was enjoying his conversation and company. You could feel it from the way he said that he was serious and in charge.

Of course, this is the same magnetism, his genuine and sincere charisma, the same intensity, and strength of personality that draws Bruce Lee's fans to the screen, time and time again. Bruce's audiences can feel his energy and his sincerity that he is a genuine person through the screen. Not just a martial arts actor, Bruce was a genuine person and an extremely rare personality. Bruce is still admired around the world today. I truly believe he will be remembered forever because people can never forget him.

Fun Being with Bruce

What I miss most about Bruce was the fun we had. Bruce occasionally showed us a couple of his favorite takedown moves, such as the wrist locks from aikido and leg sweeps that he demonstrated at the Long

Beach tournaments. He even jokingly used them as punishment when I would tease him. "OK, you are the best, but can you do this?" as I squatted toward the ground with my heels touching the ground. Bruce could not do this. He would signal for me to stand in front of him, then twist my wrist while sweeping my leg. Then he would grin and ask me, "How do you like this?" He knew I was just playing with him. After class, I would be rolling on the ground from laughter in Bruce's home office from his never-ending jokes. He was a master at setting up a joke and then delivering the punchline.

Bruce's Jokes

"Many men smoke and many men drink, but Fu Man Chu."

"I have a rich voice. It's well-off."

<u>Emperor Looking for a Bodyguard.</u>
The Japanese emperor is searching for a personal bodyguard and orders a competition be held all over Japan. When the final three samurai are selected, they are to each demonstrate their skill in front of the emperor.

The first samurai comes to the center, ready and armed. The emperor's guard has a small box that is opened, and a fly is released. The samurai draws his sword and cuts through the air. The fly is cut in half. The audience was impressed, and they all clapped.

The emperor signals the crowd to settle down. The second samurai steps up and another guard opens the small box, and another fly is released. The samurai draws his sword and cuts it twice. The fly is cut into four pieces. This time, the audience wildly cheers and applauds.

After a few minutes, the emperor signals again to calm the crowd. The third samurai steps into the center, and the last guard releases a fly from the small box. The third samurai quickly draws his sword and slices his sword through the air. But the fly was still flying! The audience is stunned. The emperor says, "The second samurai is the winner." The third samurai immediately says, "Wait," and he catches the fly with his hand, shows it to the emperor, and says, "The fly is circumcised!"

Our happy days

20

STRUGGLING IN HOLLYWOOD

When I was in Hong Kong, there was a movie titled *There's No Business Like Show Business* and a song with the same title. I always remember that line, and that inspired me to be in show business. Unfortunately, show business also is the dirtiest business.

After *The Green Hornet* was canceled, Bruce had a hard time getting to work. First, there were not a lot of roles for Asian actors. Second, those that were available were parts playing caricatures of Asian people, with pigtails and subservient behavior. They were insulting roles, and Bruce refused to accept them. This became a financial burden on Bruce and his family, especially when he hurt his back and could not even teach private lessons.

Bruce's philosophy on making movies was like his teaching of martial arts. If he did not like you, it did not matter how much you offered him, he would not teach you. Likewise, if Bruce did not think the script was good, it did not matter how much you offered him, he would not do it. Money was not what Bruce was after. He once said to me, "You must enjoy what you are doing. And if you do it well, the money will eventually come." Bruce was a man of principle, and he would never break his principles or violate his beliefs.

A favorite poster of Bruce's was the one with vultures in the desert saying, "Patience my ass! I'm gonna kill something!" This indicated a sense of Bruce's personality about waiting in Hollywood.

Bruce worked his butt off, coming up with ideas like *The Warrior* and *The Silent Flute* with Stirling Silliphant and James Coburn. Bruce was ready, but Hollywood was not ready for him.

Once, Bruce and I talked about why there was never an Asian on the theater marquee and why Caucasians portrayed oriental roles in the movies back then. Bruce was told from a Hollywood connection, "No American woman would dream of an Asian lover when they are sleeping."

Yet Bruce never discussed being discriminated against. Perhaps it was blind ambition. Bruce and I were both foreigners in a foreign land. We were both in show business, and this was a business decision. Yes, there were not many roles for the Chinese in Hollywood. Yes, there were Caucasians portraying Chinese roles. At the time, Bruce was not marketable or bankable in the eyes of Hollywood executives and producers. As Bruce said in the Pierre Berton interview, "Businesswise, it is a risk. And I do not blame them. If I were the man with the money, I probably would have my own worries if the acceptance would be there."

Racism or no racism, Bruce would be undeterred by his ambition. He was driven and determined to succeed. Bruce told me, "If Muhammed doesn't come to you, you go to Muhammed." My friend Victor Lam, whom Bruce kicked while holding the air shield, arranged for me to meet with director Chang Cheh (張徹) in late 1968 during a two-day trip to Hong Kong. At the time, Chang Cheh was on par with Lo Wei when it came to Hong Kong Chinese classical martial arts films. He was with the Shaw Brothers, and he offered Bruce $5,000 per movie. When I went back to Los Angeles and told him, Bruce declined the offer because it was too low.

After Bruce's demonstration on a Hong Kong television show, when he broke a board with a one-inch punch and smashed a couple of boards with his side kick, there was a lot of interest in Bruce abroad. It was that demonstration that director Lo Wei's son caught and mentioned to producer Raymond Chow and urged him to seek out Bruce for movies. Raymond Chow was formerly with the Shaw Brothers and wanted to break out on his own. He approached Bruce and a two-picture deal was signed.

No American woman would dream of an
Asian lover when they are sleeping.

No support behind the boards. 　　Bruce's signature side kick power, breaking five boards without any support.

21

SUCCESS AND LONELINESS IN HONG KONG

When Bruce returned to Hong Kong, I guess you could say history was made. *The Big Boss* (aka *Fists of Fury*) was a smashing success, so *Fist of Fury* (aka *The Chinese Connection*) closely followed.

There were rumors that Bruce was to star in a classic gung fu movie with Run Run Shaw. During a phone call with Bruce, he briefly mentioned a movie idea that would be based on one of the chapters from the Three Kingdoms novels in which he would portray one of the generals, 趙子龍 Zhao Zilong, who saved the emperor's infant son from 10,000 enemy soldiers. It so happened that the general's name also contained the character for dragon. When Bruce told me that, I said, "Wow, that would be a great movie. It would fit you perfectly." Just imagine the action that would have involved Bruce fighting 10,000 enemy soldiers!

After the smashing success of his first two films, Bruce decided to form Concord Productions so he could be compensated for his worth. I recall Bruce telling me that Raymond Chow tried to con him into a partnership with 51 percent for Raymond and 49 percent for Bruce. Afterward, Bruce told him, "You need me more than I need you." It would be an equal 50-50 partnership. This company would produce Bruce's next film *The Way of the Dragon* (aka *Return of the Dragon*). Bruce not only acted but also wrote the script, choreographed its fight scenes, and directed the movie. In that film, Bruce fought Chuck Norris in the classic fight scene at the Colosseum in Rome. *The Way of the Dragon* was near and dear to Bruce's heart. I recall Bruce saying how he liked the scene at the airport restroom when he was squatting on the toilet. That was a scene for the Hong Kong locals to illustrate a side of Bruce's character being a country bumpkin.

Back to Los Angeles for Medical Evaluation

Shortly after he collapsed in Hong Kong on May 10, 1973, Bruce came back to Los Angeles for a medical evaluation. During this stay, we had lunch at The Beverly Hills Hotel with Fred Weintraub to discuss having Lalo Schifrin do the soundtrack for *Enter the Dragon*. Schifrin composed the theme for the *Mission: Impossible* series as well as the movie *Bullitt*. Bruce liked that suggestion, so Bruce and I met with Schifrin to seal the deal.

Bruce stayed at one of the bungalows at the Beverly Hills Hotel, but he did not feel like going out for dinner that evening, so I asked, "What do you feel like?" Bruce mentioned the Mandarin Chinese food at a restaurant we used to go to. I offered to pick up some food to go. I remembered some of the dishes Bruce liked and ordered shredded beef with fish taste, chicken in egg white, yang chow fried rice and minced pork with vermicelli. We had a feast at the hotel with the Chinese takeout. After dinner, Bruce and I chatted. He said, "Peter, I did not forget that you like show business. If there is a part in the future that requires a mute, I will use you", and we both laughed. I do have a problem with language. I began speaking English in Australia, and even today, I still have an accent.

Visiting Bruce in Hong Kong

After Bruce finished *Way of the Dragon*, I visited him for a couple of days in Hong Kong. I went to his house in Kowloon Tong, and when I walked into the house, Dan Inosanto was walking up the stairs and Bruce told Dan, "Go ahead and prepare for tomorrow's fight scene." Bruce told Dan to work on his techniques for tomorrow's fight scene and Bruce would just fit in with him during the shoot. Dan knocked his head and he looked tired. This was Bruce's way of unscripted choreography, a true master.

Bruce showed me a bamboo stick and said that he was going to use it as a weapon. He played around with it in front of me. Many years later, I realized it was the bamboo stick he used in *Game of Death* in the fight scene with Dan.

Kareem had already filmed his fight sequence with Bruce for *Game of Death* and returned to the States. Bruce compensated him with several custom-tailored suits. Hong Kong is known for its custom-made suits. I can only imagine what the tailor in fabric took to make Kareem's long pants!

I proceeded to walk with Bruce to his bedroom where he showed me his new toys, which were cameras. Bruce really enjoyed photography.

Bruce talked about wanting to make a Western movie during the period when the Chinese were working on the railroads. He mentioned working on a new script, and he really liked the title 南拳北腿 Northern Leg, Southern Fist. They are the two main categories of Chinese gung fu. We did not talk much about that script except the title as he made a few moves with his legs and hands while he smiled.

The next day, we went to lunch with Raymond Chow and some executives of Golden Harvest. We had shark fin soup, and I placed an order for yang chow fried rice. Everyone was surprised that I ordered it, but Bruce gave me an eyewink because he knew what was going on. When the shark fin soup and fried rice arrived, I mixed the fried rice into my bowl of shark fin, and I passed it on to Bruce. Everyone looked at us in disbelief. In those days, shark fin soup was a delicacy, and it was not proper to mix it with anything else. But Bruce and I liked it that way. Later, it became popular in Hong Kong: shark fin soup with fried rice. I also discovered Bruce's new favorite drink: ginger beer. Bruce did not drink, so when a waiter asked if he would like a drink, he would ask, "How about a ginger beer?" He made it sound cool!

When we went shopping, I knew a friend who owned a boutique with Japanese-made clothing. I knew Bruce would like the boutique's style and design, so we went there. He ended up buying a few jackets, and he bought me one, too.

That night, Bruce invited me to a Japanese restaurant for dinner. The restaurant owner was a big fan of Bruce's. Even though only two days passed, we had a great time talking, joking, laughing, and, most importantly, communicating with each other. It is not easy to find someone who can really understand you and be able to empathize and communicate without saying a word.

The Cost of Success

With the huge success of his movies, Bruce was mobbed by the public. He said, "The biggest disadvantage of success is losing your privacy." Bruce had to jog in the morning on the streets of Hong Kong because the fans would not let him get his workout in.

The news media was also relentless on Bruce's celebrity status. Because anything about Bruce was newsworthy, the press took potshots at him and fed the public's appetite. Bruce really hated all kinds of gossip in the Hong Kong newspapers.

Even worse, Bruce had few friends in Hong Kong. There was a trust issue because people continually wanted to take advantage of him. During this period, Bruce said in an interview that the term "friend" had become a scarce word. True, trusted friends were hard to come by for Bruce.

All things considered; I do not blame Bruce for wanting to return to the United States. For Bruce, it was "family first." He would never leave his family. Linda wanted to raise Brandon and Shannon in the States, and I believe Bruce agreed with her. I truly believe the main reasons Bruce wanted to go back to the States were for work opportunities and greater privacy.

My Last Conversations with Bruce

After Bruce finished *Enter the Dragon,* we talked over the phone five days before he passed away. I was in Las Vegas. During that conversation, we planned for me to go to Hong Kong for two days and come back with Bruce to the U.S. to promote *Enter the Dragon.* The first promotion would be on *The Tonight Show with Johnny Carson.*

Bruce was very happy with the way *Enter the Dragon* turned out. He mentioned some of the scenes he particularly liked, such as "the art of fighting without fighting" on the boat to Han's Island and the banquet scene when he tells John Saxon, "Don't con me."

He mentioned having a hard time finding good martial artists to fight him in the next movie. He had to find high-level martial artists for the fight scenes to be good. Even though it is just a movie, it would be bad for their reputation and interfere with their student enrollment. "It takes two to tango," and those high-level masters would know they would not be able to be the winner. Many turned down his movie offers.

He was already thinking about his next movie. He said that there were so many offers from different studios and independent producers to produce his next movies and that it seemed like everyone wanted something. During that conversation, Bruce sounded tired and extremely lonely. After we hung up, I felt something was wrong with Bruce by the tone of his voice. I wish I could have gone back to Hong Kong immediately.

Five days later, I received a call from Linda, "Hi, Peter. I want you to know Bruce passed away yesterday." "What?" I spoke. Linda answered, "Yes, Bruce passed away." I was shocked and speechless. I banged myself against the wall, wishing I had flown to Hong Kong right after Bruce and I spoke a few days ago. I told Linda, "I am taking the next flight out to Hong Kong."

Bruce in Chinese traditional costume and weapons.

Bruce bought me the same jacket as a gift.

My last conversation with Bruce.

Signed movie contract with Andrew G. Vajna-
later executive producer for Rambo and Terminator.

22

THE AFTERMATH

When I went to Hong Kong for Bruce's funeral, I was hoping to help Linda, but instead, Linda had to help me. The devastation of losing Bruce was almost unbearable, and the strength Linda possessed was amazing. After visiting Linda at their home, I went to the funeral parlor where Bruce was. When I saw Bruce's body, I broke down. Actress Nora Miao was there, and she comforted me.

I must admit that the funeral in Hong Kong was a blur. I was overwhelmed by the crowds that were outside the funeral parlor. The newspapers reported that there were 25,000 people, but I believe there were many, many more. In the beginning, I was sitting right behind Linda, but I was overcome with grief, so I made my way to the back of the funeral parlor. It was hot and humid, and I remember the burning of incense.

After the funeral in Hong Kong, I flew to Seattle for Bruce's second funeral. The day before, Linda called me and requested that I be one of the pallbearers. Truthfully, I did not even know what a pallbearer was, it was such an honor to be one of the pallbearers. The pallbearers included actors Steve McQueen and James Coburn, students Taky Kimura and Dan Inosanto, and Bruce's brother Robert.

During the ceremony, I recall sitting in the back with Dan and Taky. We were all crying. The atmosphere was somber, dead silence.

Everyone was in a state of shock. I recall hearing *And When I Die* by Blood, Sweat & Tears. The last song was Bruce's favorite — *My Way* by Frank Sinatra. The lyrics speak for themselves; it was a fitting tribute to Bruce.

The press was relentless when Bruce passed away. A news story was in the newspaper every day, the more sensational the better. As I said, show business can be the dirtiest business. Since I went back to Hong Kong for Bruce's funeral and I could speak Cantonese, I became a paper celebrity, constantly in the newspapers with reporters interviewing and quoting me. As a result, I was having my own battle with the press.

While in Hong Kong for the funeral, a movie producer from Los Angeles, Andrew Vajna, knocked on my hotel door. He approached me about starring in a martial arts movie. The script had not yet been written, but he offered me a $15,000 retainer. I must admit that the timing was odd, but I had more faith in the movie producers in the U.S. than I did for those in Hong Kong, especially with what Bruce experienced. After the funeral in Seattle, I returned to Hong Kong to see whether the picture could be made.

Who was going to be the next Bruce Lee? Who was going to replace Bruce? Those were the questions the press wanted to know. When word got out that I might possibly be in a martial arts movie, I was branded as "making dead man's money." As soon as I heard that, I was out. There was no way I would profit off Bruce's name or death. I was done and left Hong Kong.

I was still grieving from Bruce's passing, so I returned to Seattle for a month to help Linda, but truthfully, she continued to help me. It rained in Seattle every day that month, adding to my depression.

After that month, I returned to Las Vegas to start my new job. Linda took me to the airport, and on the way, she said to me, "Peter, not everyone can be like Bruce. He possessed a few ingredients that not everyone has. He had a photographic memory, he knew human anatomy, and he knew how to take care of his temple "body" with nutrition." Linda's words about Bruce stayed with me to this day.

Funeral in Hong Kong

Funeral in Seattle

> My Definite Chief Aim
>
> I, Bruce Lee, will be the first highest paid Oriental super star in the United States. In return I will give the most exciting performances and render the best of quality in the capacity of an actor. Starting 1970 I will achieve world fame and from then onwards till the end of 1980 I will have in my possession $10,000,000. I will live the way I please and achieve inner harmony and happiness.
>
> Bruce Lee
> Jan 1969

When I read that letter, I said to myself, "Wow! Bruce was really deep."

While I was in Hong Kong immediately after Bruce passed away, Linda showed me a small booklet. It was in Bruce's briefcase, and she told me that he read it every day and that she would like me to have it. I saw this book before when Bruce first showed it to me back in 1968. It is the poem *If* by Rudyard Kipling. It indicated what Bruce must have been going through during that time.

IF
by
Rudyard Kipling

If you can keep your head when all about you
Are losing theirs and blaming it on you,
If you can trust yourself when all men doubt you,
But make allowance for their doubting too.
If you can wait and not be tired by waiting,
Or being lied about, don't deal in lies,
Or being hated, don't give way to hating,
And yet don't look too good, nor talk too wise:

If you can dream — and not make dreams your master.
If you can think — and not make thoughts your aim.
If you can meet with Triumph and Disaster
And treat those two impostors just the same.
If you can bear to hear the truth you've spoken
Twisted by knaves to make a trap for fools,
Or watch the things you gave your life to, broken,
And stoop and build 'em up with worn-out tools:

If you can make one heap of all your winnings
And risk it on one turn of pitch-and-toss,
And lose and start again at your beginnings.
And never breathe a word about your loss.
If you can force your heart and nerve and sinew
To serve your turn long after they are gone,
And so, hold on when there is nothing in you.
Except the Will which says to them: 'Hold on!'

If you can talk with crowds and keep your virtue,
Or walk with Kings — nor lose the common touch,
If neither foes nor loving friends can hurt you,
If all men count with you, but none too much.
If you can fill the unforgiving minute
With sixty seconds' worth of distance run,
Yours is the Earth and everything that's in it,
And — which is more — you'll be a Man, my son!

Ever since Bruce passed away, IF has helped me a lot and I still read it occasionally. It is really inspiring. I encourage people to read it because it is a very powerful poem. Its meaning changes or reveals something new every time I read it. Reading it again six months later, it will have a different meaning. My favorite line is, "If you can dream — and not make dreams your master."

I did not continue training in martial arts after Bruce passed away. I went into a deep depression for many years because I missed him a lot. Instead of physical training, I have used his philosophy in my daily life, including my business. Reflecting on the last 50 years since Bruce's passing, I realize that it was Bruce's philosophy that is enduring. Yes, he was at the pinnacle of physical fitness and a fierce fighter, but like yin and yang, his inspirational words are still with us and influencing generations.

Even today, Bruce's name and his teachings always come up. Bruce motivates not just jeet kune do practitioners but also martial artists from all styles. Fans of Bruce are continually wowed by his films. Bruce said, "One will learn something every day and there is no end to it." It is exactly like Bruce said, "Running water never goes stale, so you got to just keep on flowing." You learn something every day.

Over time, I moved on. I settled in Las Vegas and married the love of my life, my spouse and life partner Sandy. We had two daughters, Jade and Crystal, and became grandparents to their children, Amelia and Jaden.

My uncle, John Lieu, told me it would be better to get into the casino business than work in a restaurant, so I started at the bottom of the casino business as a shill, just like in the restaurant business washing dishes. A shill is someone hired by the casino to pose as a customer to decoy others and convince them to gamble. Later, I became a baccarat dealer, which was difficult in those days. You would either must be a casino manager's son or friend to get a good-paying job. The salary was low, but the tips were great. Later, I continued to use a few of Bruce's basic philosophies, and I kept moving on to better jobs in the casino business.

In 1980, I saved enough money and started a restaurant business yet remained in the casino business as a casino junketeer, who brings customers to the casino for a commission. During that time, I was lucky to meet a couple of Chinese high rollers. I never told anyone that I was Bruce Lee's student but someone else would. A player would ask their friends, "Who is Peter?" and they would answer, "Peter was Bruce Lee's student." Suddenly, the players would feel comfortable with me and have me hang around with them. They felt like they could trust me. Through two Chinese players, I got to meet certain countries' presidents, a Vatican official, and even the Shaolin abbot. They all seemed comfortable once they heard I was Bruce's student. It's just amazing how different heads of state all have such respect for Bruce. Later, I taught myself about the reverse merger business using Bruce's philosophies by asking people.

Linda gave me the poem IF when I went back to Hong Kong
for Bruce's funeral. Linda told me that Bruce carried
with him in his briefcase every day.

24

WHY DID BRUCE GIVE ME A JKD CERTIFICATE?

The date on the jeet kune do certificate is August 14, 1968, two days before my birthday when Bruce handed it to me. The truth is that I was shocked when I received the certificate. Bruce was smiling and he winked when pointing to the line stating, "Personally taught by Bruce Lee." He gave me first rank, but the rank means nothing to me because I know Bruce really did not believe in ranking. Even one with a higher ranking does not mean one truly understands Bruce's teaching. I was simply honored that Bruce recognized my achievement in jeet kune do.

I wonder how Bruce came to give it to me, especially after understanding that Bruce issued this kind of certificate to only a handful of people. At the same time, I ask myself, "Would Bruce give someone a certificate who doesn't deserve it?" I do not think so.

I estimate receiving approximately 110 hours of training with Bruce. In my opinion, Bruce noticed that with everything he showed me, I picked up his teaching quickly. Most importantly, I believe that Bruce recognized my understanding of his philosophy of martial arts through our many conversations after workouts in his library. Because of our shared backgrounds of being raised in Hong Kong, we shared the Chinese culture, language, and martial arts philosophies from the Hong Kong martial arts storybooks of the 1950s, a common bond that played a very important part in both our lives. We both believed in the maxims of respecting the elderly, taking care of our family, and not having our spouses work because it is the husband's job to provide for the family. In many ways, what we learned from martial arts would be lessons in life.

Bruce also never charged me a penny for lessons. He taught the Hollywood stars and when I told him I could not afford lessons, Bruce took me in and taught me as a friend. He knew that I would do anything for him. For sure, I would take a bullet for him.

Lately, the term "friend" has become a scarce word, especially when combined with loyalty. Bruce still teaches me today, and I will remain loyal to him for the rest of my life.

A Friend Forever in My Heart

There is one thing I must mention to understand why Bruce means so much to me. Bruce is the only person I know who never changed. From the day I first met him to when I officially started training with him in late 1967 to the last phone call with him in 1973, he treated me the same way. When I first met Bruce, I was working as a busboy. When Bruce reached superstar status, every time I called, he would pick up the phone and we just talked like back in the days after class. He was the same Bruce. It is almost impossible to find someone you can call a friend and they do not change in some way toward you.

One is lucky to have such a friend in your lifetime. This might be your spouse. But if you could have more than one, someone who really understands you and communicates with you, without saying a word, you would be extremely lucky.

One night, Bruce had this small book he was reading and said to me, "This is a good little book. When you are having a good time, you really do not realize it until you leave — when the party's over. And then you say, 'I just had a great time.'

Since I met Bruce back in December 1963 until today, there is not one day that I have not thought about him. It is hard to describe. In 1973, Bruce returned to Los Angeles for his physical checkup. I had not seen him for almost a year even though we spoke on the phone occasionally. Bruce knew I missed him. When we were in an elevator to Adrian Marshall's office (Bruce's personal attorney), he said to me, "Friends don't need to see each other all the time; it's in the heart." Yes, I was Bruce Lee's last disciple, and he is in my heart every day.

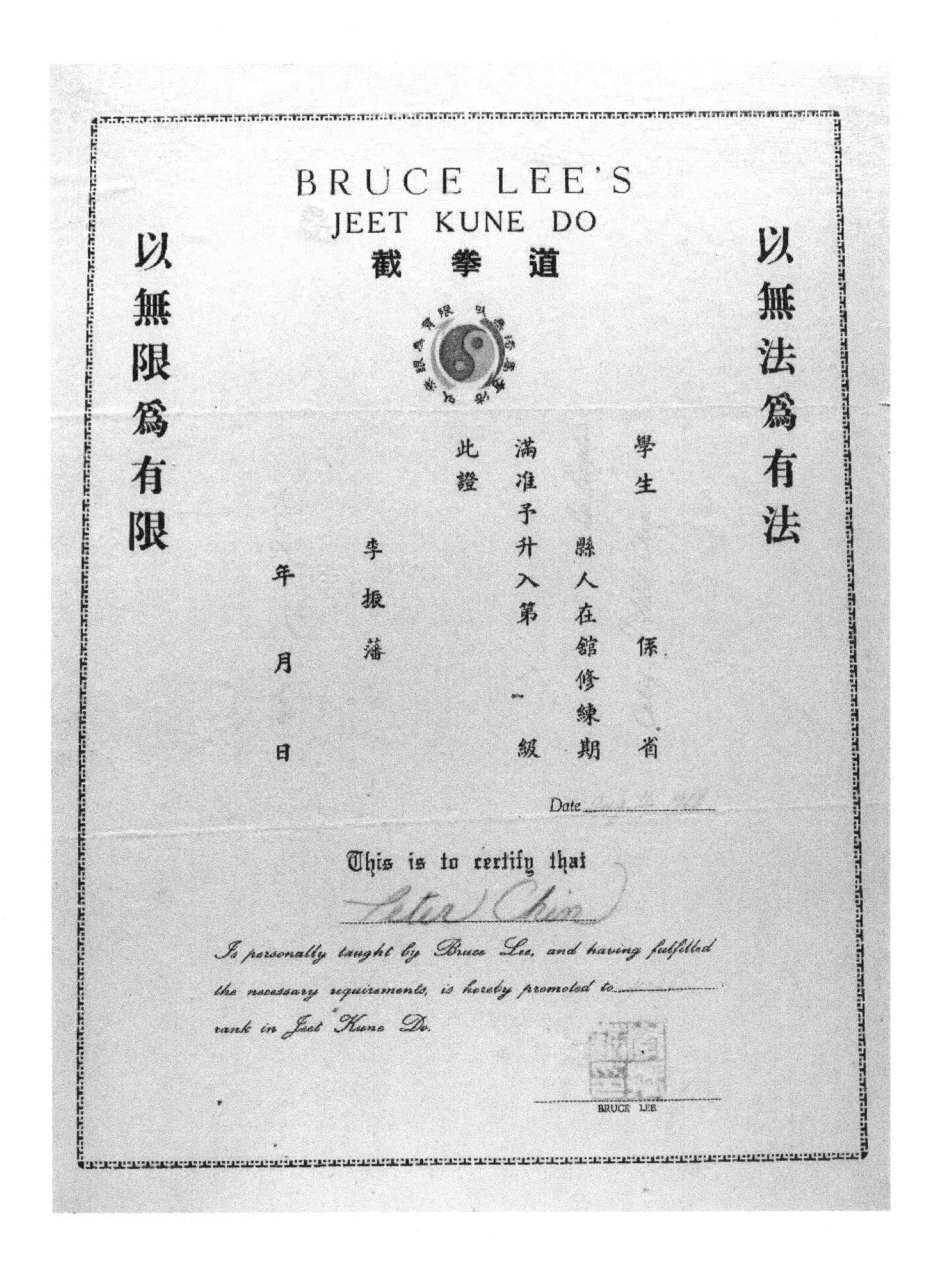

BRUCE LEE'S
JEET KUNE DO
截拳道

以無限爲有限

以無法爲有法

學生

係

縣人在館修練期

省

滿准予升入第

此證

李振藩

一級

年月日

Date

This is to certify that

Peter Chin

Is personally taught by Bruce Lee, and having fulfilled the necessary requirements, is hereby promoted to_____ rank in Jeet Kune Do.

BRUCE LEE

CONCLUSION: BRUCE'S TRUE SECRET

In conclusion, please understand that all styles of martial arts are good, but you must put in the time and effort to be good. Be "out of the box" and be open-minded to new things. Even tai chi exercise can be of great value as we age. Understand that martial arts are first for health and second for self-defense, so you must put in the physical effort with training and conditioning the body before gaining any benefit. While honing your techniques is important, remember that it is a daily decrease and not an increase. Do not neglect your jogging and abdominal exercises, and treat your body as a temple through study, knowledge, and proper nutrition.

I want to encourage people to continue to study Bruce's words. Read and value Bruce's words until you can understand and use his philosophy to help yourself grow and follow whatever path you choose. Develop your character with honesty and integrity and have the discipline and commitment to your personal growth. Be like water and persevere through life's storms because I can guarantee that you will experience them, so adapt to life's ever-changing circumstances and overcome them.

On the next page, the true secret to Bruce Lee's jeet kune do and personal philosophy is revealed to the reader. Remember that two heads are better than one, but the next page exemplifies the true meaning and source of self-help and the axiom, "What you put in is what you are going to get out."

It all depends on yourself

SELFHELP

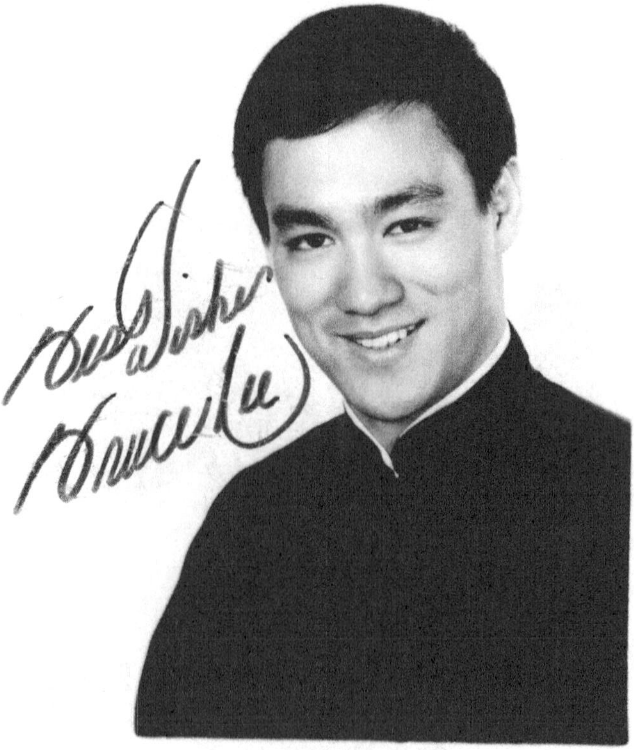
Best Wishes
Bruce Lee

ACKNOWLEDGMENTS

I want to express my deepest gratitude to my editorial team: Rosemary Gong and Jeff Pisciotta. Without them, I would not be able to express myself clearly because English is my second language. Grateful acknowledgements are extended to David Tadman, an esteemed collector and historian of Bruce Lee, for his generous contribution of images for the book. I would also like to credit Greg Rhodes for his valuable chronology of Bruce Lee, and express my appreciation to Steve Kerridge, another notable Bruce Lee historian, for his introduction to Greg Rhodes and provision of additional pictures. I want to express my deep appreciation to my daughter Jade, for designing the book cover. Without her invaluable assistance, I would not have been able to publish the book.

I attribute at least half of Bruce's success to Linda Lee Cadwell. She was the rock in Bruce's life, keeping him centered through all the trials and tribulations they encountered. Linda was yin to Bruce's yang. Linda provided the support and encouragement Bruce needed to carry on with the challenges in his life, such as his debilitating back injury and dealing with Hollywood. I know Bruce felt extremely fortunate to have Linda by his side. She was the supportive force behind Bruce's legacy. Although we have not seen each other often, my relationship with Linda has remained strong over all these years. As Bruce told me, "Friends don't need to see each other all the time; it's in the heart." She has kept Bruce's legacy alive and passed it down to their daughter Shannon.

In the same way, I am blessed with my Sandy. I would not be half the man I am without her. I am incredibly grateful to have gone through life together with my Sandy.

— Peter Chin

I would like to thank Peter Chin for sharing his memories of Bruce Lee with me. He showed me a different side of Bruce and the significance of Chinese philosophy and culture in Chinese martial arts. Without them, practitioners are soulless and missing all that heavenly glory.

— Tommy Gong

Made in the USA
Las Vegas, NV
14 February 2024